Facing Strategic Issues:
New Planning Guides and Practices

by Rochelle O'Connor

A Research Report from The Conference Board

Contents

	Page
About This Report	iv
Why This Report	v
Introduction	vi
1. **The Major Issues**	1
The Economy	1
Productivity and Quality	2
Technology, Innovation, Expansion	2
Deregulation, Energy, International Competition	3
2. **Planning Procedures and Techniques**	5
Time Horizon	5
Planning Calendar	6
Strategic Presentations and Reviews	7
Competitive Intelligence	9
Computers and Computer Models	12
Portfolio Management Approach	13
Avoiding Surprise: Forecasts, Assumptions, Scenarios, Contingency Planning	14
Focusing on Strategic Issues	20
Some Other Changes and Nonchanges	21
Planning for Staff and Support Units	21
Planning Internationally	24
Monitoring the Plan	24
3. **Planning Documentation and Formats**	25

Exhibits

1. Profiles of Major Expansion and Development Proposals—A Construction Company	4	5. Major Areas to Be Covered In Plan Presentations—A Diversified Manufacturer	8
2. Timetable for Strategic Plans—An Information Services Corporation	6	6. Instructions for Preparation for Plan Review Meetings—A Newspaper Publisher	9
3. Planning Calendar—An Industrial Products Corporation	7	7. Instructions for Competitive Environment Analysis—An Industrial Equipment Manufacturer	11
4. Planning Process—A Forest Products and Paper Corporation	7	8. Format for Competitive Analysis—A Food Products Company	12

9. Business Classification Explanations—An Engineering and Construction Firm 13
10. Business Unit Phases of Strategy—A Diversified Manufacturer 14
11. Strategic Analysis of Strategic Business Units—A Chemical Company 15
12. Instructions for Environmental Assumptions—An Industrial Products Company 17
13. Contingency Plans Instructions—An Industrial Products Manufacturer 19
14. Contingency Planning Instructions—An Insurance Firm 19
15. Instructions for Threats and Opportunities/Contingency Plans—A Machine and Tool Manufacturer 20
16. Instructions for Issue Resolution—A Steel Company 22
17. Function Responsibilities and Plans Required—A Diversified Company 23
18. A New Emphasis in the Planning Process—A Diversified Machinery Manufacturer 27
19. Practical Exercises for the Manager—A Diversified Machinery Manufacturer 28

Contents of Planning Manuals

20. Contents of Planning Manual—A Packaging Manufacturer 30
21. Long-Range Strategic Plan—A Computer Hardware and Services Company 30

Plan Outlines and Contents

22. Components of Planning System—A Medical Products Firm 32
23. Plan Outline—An Industrial Products Manufacturer .. 32
24. Plan Contents—A Transportation Company 32
25. Plan Outline—A High-Technology Products Manufacturer 32

Executive Summary

26. One-Page Plan Summary—An Industrial Products Manufacturer 33
27. Executive Comment—An Information Services Corporation 33
28. Executive Summary—A Construction Company 34
29. Executive Summary—An Industrial Products Firm .. 34

Mission Statement

30. Mission Statement—An Insurance Company 35
31. Mission Statement—A Telecommunications Company 35

External Analysis

32. External Situation Analysis—An Industrial Products Manufacturer 36
33. External Trends and Analysis—A Toiletries and Cosmetics Firm 36
34. Market Analysis Instructions—A Bank Holding Company 37
35. Situation Analysis—An Industrial Products Manufacturer 38

Internal Analysis

36. Situation Analysis—A Pharmaceuticals Company ... 39
37. Internal Analysis—An Industrial Products Manufacturer 40
38. Internal Analysis—A Medical Products Firm 41

Goals and Objectives

39. Strategic Objectives—A Diversified Machinery Manufacturer 41
40. Strategic Objectives—An Industrial Equipment Company 42
41. Strategic Objectives—A Computer Hardware and Services Corporation 43

Strategies

42. Statement of Strategy—A Diversified Industrial Equipment Corporation 44
43. Strategy Checklist—A Packaging Manufacturer 44
44. Statement of Strategy—A Food Company 47

Action Programs

45. Action Plans—A Consumer and Industrial Products Company 48
46. Action Plans—A Machinery and Tool Manufacturer 49
47. Action Plan Summary—A Building Products Company 50

About This Report

THIS REPORT updates a Conference Board report published in 1976, when many companies were still establishing a planning system and developing instructions, guides and manuals to direct the planning process.[1] Since then, most companies have experienced many changes in their managements, their businesses, markets and competition. This study explores what companies have done through their planning systems to respond to their changed business environments.

The companies participating in this study were asked what principal changes they had made over the past five years affecting: (1) the substance and issues of plans, and (2) the planning procedures and documents. A total of 214 companies responded to a questionnaire survey. Of these, 115 submitted copies of company planning instructions, guides and manuals, from which exhibits were selected.

[1] Rochelle O'Connor, *Corporate Guides to Long-Range Planning*. The Conference Board, Report No. 687, 1976.

Companies Participating in This Study

Size of Companies by Sales or Revenues	Manufacturing	Non-manufacturing	Total Companies Number	Percent
Under $1 billion	35	25	60	28
$1 billion to $5 billion	60	42	102	48
Over $5 billion	24	27	51	24
Total[1]	119	94	213	100

Median: $1.814 billion

[1] One company did not report this information

Type of Business	Number of Companies
Manufacturing	
Industrial products	51
Consumer products	24
Both types of products	37
Not specified	7
Total	119 (56%)
Nonmanufacturing	
Financial	29
Utility	14
Mining	13
Wholesale and retail	12
Transportation	5
Communications	5
Other	17
Total	95 (44%)

Why This Report

MANAGING CHANGE is the most critical challenge facing management today. Pulled by the equally strong forces of current operational needs and future strategic direction, corporate managements have to make critical decisions *now* for both today and tomorrow. Strategic planning is meant to harness present demands to a vision of the future.

Because developing realistic and implementable strategies in a constantly changing world is a task requiring the best managerial competence, effective planning must take advantage of managers' knowledge, experience and judgment. To this end, it depends as heavily on information gathering as on decision making.

The planning procedures and documents discussed in this report are but the visible trappings of the process, but they furnish the kind of guidance that is needed to develop the best strategy for the firm.

The Conference Board is grateful to the 214 planners who generously shared their companies' planning experiences and documents that serve as the basis of this study.

JAMES T. MILLS
President

Introduction

FOR MOST COMPANIES, learning how to plan strategically—not as an academic exercise but in a way that is both practical and tailored to the actual business needs of the company—has been an evolutionary process taking place over many years. This report documents the latest developments in that evolution, examining current thinking and practice in the design of company strategic planning systems. It is intended to inform those who are principally responsible for strategic planning in their companies, and it tells the story mainly from the corporate planners' point of view. Many of them believe the function has been in a state of change from its very inception.

What is the nature of the changes that beset the planning process? They generally reflect the refinement of the discipline needed to develop strategies. They also take into account the kaleidoscopic forces that significantly influence those strategies. The changes affect a process that is basically meant to establish a framework for:

(1) Asking the right questions;
(2) Gathering the essential information;
(3) Analyzing the relevant data;
(4) Developing strategic options; and
(5) Selecting the appropriate strategy.

Evolution takes different forms in different organizations: from adoption of new sophisticated techniques and methodologies to more intense analysis of competition and markets; from a rescheduled planning calendar to an examination of the global environment. The intent remains constant: to respond to the elements of the planning framework in the best possible way; to provide the best strategy for the firm.

Most apparent in this survey of strategic planners in 214 companies is their awareness of, and renewed application to addressing the critical strategic issues that face their companies, and their attempts to provide a planning system that will facilitate this process. To this end, the companies participating in this study indicate that they are pursuing, in the main, three principal avenues:

(1) More focused communication and dialogue with line managers aimed at getting the right questions, as well as the right answers, on the table.

(2) A greater degree of procedural flexibility and informality designed to draw all units and levels into a more effective participation.

(3) A drive to simplify requirements and to eliminate what experience has proven to be unproductive paperwork.

This survey shows a continuing management commitment to develop effective strategies for positioning the company in new changing environments and meeting competitive challenges. The heightened sensibility to respond to the needs imposed by outside forces, as well as the firm's internal ethos, is evidenced in the continuing evolution and change in the strategic-planning process.

This study looks at the principal changes that companies have made over the past five years in: (1) the kinds of issues they have to address in their plans; (2) the planning procedures designed to do this more effectively; and (3) the instructions, guides and formats used to document the development of strategy.

Evolution in Company Planning Systems

The evolutionary nature of company planning is indicated by the fact that in two-thirds of the participating companies, the corporate planning unit has been in existence for more than five years. However, the present planning system is less than five years old in more than half of the companies represented. Further, while a quarter of the units are more than ten years old, only 13 percent of the systems are of that age.

Chapter 1

The Major Issues

EVERY INDUSTRY and every company feels the impact of external factors differently. The problems of those with mature products and services cannot be compared realistically with those scrambling for a foothold in newly emerging businesses. Nevertheless, there are some issues that affect nearly all companies' efforts in one way or another. These are the major broad issues that form the context for planning for most U.S. businesses.

The Economy

Economic conditions and their related consequences, as might be expected, are of primary concern to more than half of the 214 companies participating in this survey. Such factors as inflation, volatile interest rates, and the availability or cost of capital are major influences that must be taken into account when developing strategies. The seeming unpredictability of these factors even further complicates attempts to resolve them.

The survey respondents report that over the past five years some immediate responses have had to be made, and these significantly influence the company's future planning. The principal measures taken to respond to financial pressures are:

(1) *Tighter cost controls.* Over half the participating companies say that tighter cost controls have been an immediate reaction to reduced income. Limitations on spending have taken such forms as staff cuts, consolidation of units, restructuring of overhead, more stringent allocation of resources, and a general reorganization of corporate priorities

(2) *Limitations of capital expenditures.* Capital expenditures have received a more critical appraisal in many firms as interest rates, inflation and the availability of capital have altered their original plans. Under new capital-rationing programs, more careful screening has resulted in changes in investment-decision criteria, and special reviews on risk, particularly of big-ticket items.

(3) *Asset-redeployment programs.* A number of companies have reevaluated their businesses to identify less profitable units. This has led to a move, in the words of one respondent, "to get rid of the losers."

None of these steps is undertaken lightly, of course, and requires more or different kinds of analyses than some companies had used in the past. This kind of experience has generated changes in the planning procedures in many organizations to prepare them to meet such problems in the future, and to avoid surprises.

One result of this more intensive examination is a reevaluation of traditional performance criteria and measurements. Another is a reevaluation of financial objectives. Ninety-four of the surveyed companies say they have made changes in such criteria or measures. Many have shifted the emphasis they put on various rates of return. For example, there appears to be a greater focus on return on equity (ROE), particularly among the manufacturing companies. Return on investment (ROI) is the next most frequently mentioned ratio examined. In many companies, return targets have been raised; in others, new ways of calculating or showing relationships to other important factors are sought.[1]

Among the more obvious impacts that economic issues have had on many firms' planning processes:

• While multiple criteria are common in a number of companies, they are applied more flexibly, according to some of the survey respondents. In one company, for instance, the focus is on ROI at the division level, but on ROE at the corporate level.

• Another company states that ROI objectives remain, but "the operating units need not achieve them if they are not realistic for those units."

---

[1] For a discussion of financial performance criteria, see Francis J. Walsh, Jr., *Measuring Business Performance.* The Conference Board, Research Bulletin No. 153, 1984.

- Several participating planners also explain that there is now a greater recognition that the introductory stages of new products or new ventures deserve—or require—different criteria for measurement.
- In a number of cases, market share also comes under closer scrutiny.
- Internally, tougher hurdle rates have been set, several companies say, while others have changed the method of calculating internal interest-rate charges to arrive at more realistic evaluations.
- In a further effort to understand true, inflation-free results, a number of companies insist on the display of "real" numbers. In other words, current-dollar data no longer satisfy management during the review of plans in a number of firms.

Productivity and Quality

Almost half of the survey participants addressed the challenges of productivity and quality improvement. The manufacturing companies especially indicate that they have made major commitments and placed great emphasis on efforts to improve both their efficiency and their competitive standing in these areas. Not only have higher corporate priorities been given to the programs, but some companies have specifically addressed this issue in developing their strategic plans.

One company has introduced a section on productivity in its new planning format to assure greater visibility and attention to these efforts. It requests that each division cover what actions are being taken to improve productivity of materials, capital and labor during the planning period. The guide further advises:

"Attracting resources and putting them to work is only the beginning. The task of a business is to make resources productive. Every business, therefore, needs productivity objectives with respect to each of the three major resources—materials, labor and capital—and with respect to overall productivity itself.

"A productivity measurement is the best yardstick for comparing management of different units within an enterprise and for comparing managements of different enterprises. For productivity includes all the efforts the enterprise contributes; it excludes everything it does not control. Productivity is the first test of management's competence.

"The goal is not to try to find the one perfect productivity measurement but to use a *number* of measurements. At least one gains insight that way.

"We need to measure productivity in all areas by a number of yardsticks to gain insight and judgment. Labor is only one of the three factors of production. And if productivity of labor is accomplished by making the other resources less productive, there can be a loss of productivity.

"The continuous improvement of productivity is one of management's most important jobs. It is also one of the most difficult, for productivity is a balance among a diversity of factors, few of which are easily definable or clearly measurable."

Cost reduction is, of course, a primary reason for the introduction of productivity programs. The savings have been difficult to measure for many businesses, and the need to find ways to measure improvement often coincides with the need to establish methods of improvement themselves.

One company requires productivity goals to be set by the business units and staff groups; these goals are reviewed and monitored rigorously.

Quality-assurance programs have also been fostered over the past few years in several manufacturing organizations. Quality ranks equally high as a competitive factor in the service industries, and is specifically addressed in their plans.

Technology, Innovation, Expansion

All of the 84 respondents who commented on the changes in their companies' strategies for technological innovation and new products say that greater emphasis and intensified efforts are being placed in these directions. There is increased concentration on R&D in many organizations, particularly in technologies that hold the potential of entry into new markets. This focus on areas of maximum strategic impact has involved major investment decisions in some cases.

The nonmanufacturing companies in the survey represent a wide diversity of industries and have responded to a greater variety of technological developments. Communications, utilities, health-care and financial institutions, for example, are all affected by different kinds of rapidly changing technologies. In all industries, however, the search is on to develop new products and services.

Thus a number of companies encourage—or even require—innovative approaches to be documented in their plans. An industrial products firm defines its interest in "innovative strategies" by giving examples of what is meant: new products, opening new markets, new methods of distribution, new physical location, and acquisitions. These strategies, the guidelines explain, are concerned with "doing things differently." They cover such areas as:

"Risk-taking decisions: a departure from the status quo.

"Resource allocation: usually involves a major reallocation of the division's physical, human and financial resources.

"Future oriented: concerns the long range and is creative."

A computer hardware company looks at the status of innovation in one part of the internal profile of its businesses. To raise the awareness of managers to this important issue, they are requested to complete a form describing how innovation is "nurtured" and leveraged within the business.

"How do you assess the presence of innovation within your business?" the instructions ask. "Identify its 'inhibitors' and 'enablers.'"

A newspaper publishing company gives specific directions to its managers on development plans:

"That portion of the plan dealing with development should identify new opportunities (e.g., markets, products, services, or acquisitions) to be investigated or pursued by your company and should establish priorities and a structured program for evaluating and/or acting upon these situations. It should include:

"(1) A detailed analysis of all significant alternative sources of sales and profit growth, including expansion of existing product line, addition of new product, and/or entry into a new or related business. Besides identifying sources of growth, this section, whenever possible, should examine the *costs* and *benefits* of alternative development programs and their anticipated impact on overall company performance.

"(2) A status report on any current development projects showing responsibility, schedules, progress to date and estimated percentage completion, past and projected expenditures, anticipated sales and profitability, and marketing strategy.

"(3) A concise description of proposed internal development projects, including your reasons for believing them to be attractive opportunities, preliminary estimates of sales, profitability and estimated investment; and a program for evaluation of the project, together with related target dates. This section should also describe or identify the need for any sponsored research or joint ventures.

"(4) Definition of any logical areas (or specific prospects) for acquisition based on the present capabilities and/or needs of your company with respect to markets, products, distribution channels, production capacity, or management."

Profiles of major expansion and development proposals are delineated in a format provided by an engineering and construction services corporation. The instructions and the form are shown in Exhibit 1.

Most of the companies seem to focus on growth through internal development. For while acquisitions are still sought by many as a means of expanding their businesses, there is a marked decrease in the aggressive policies that were common several years ago.

The exceptions are those in newly deregulated industries that, long precluded from diversification, now seem intent on making up for lost time. Also, a number of companies long centered in a single declining industry—steel is a case in point—are also looking for acquisitions. But even these indicate that they are very selective in their criteria for acquisitions. Most report a greater concern than formerly with screening acquisition candidates in the search for growth opportunities. In many cases, formal programs have been set up to establish acquisition guidelines and criteria to ensure congruence with the firm's strategic objectives. Several companies, on the other hand, have shifted the focus on acquisitions to the operating units and a product orientation.

Deregulation, Energy, International Competition

As might be expected, those industries subject to regulation and deregulation have had to consider crucial changes of strategy. Companies in such industries as transportation, finance and utilities now face new competitors, new markets, and new opportunities.

Deregulation presents critical challenges to many managers who now have to place greater emphasis on marketing and new-product development. Regulation—such as the cost-containment measures in the health-care field—has also prodded those companies that must observe regulatory restrictions.

The cost and availability of energy is no longer the general problem it was several years ago, but 63 companies indicate that it has affected their plans. It has led to conservation efforts, more flexible energy-purchase programs, and closer monitoring of costs. For the utility companies, particularly, this is a major factor in running their businesses. In the manufacturing companies, there is an increased focus on alternative energy sources, and some companies require energy conservation to be considered in divisional plans. A few companies report that cost and availability of energy is one of the factors considered in developing multiple scenarios and contingency plans.

The competition most surveyed companies are particularly concerned about is domestic competition. Even when companies have significant foreign competitors, it is the struggle in the United States they primarily worry about. Relatively few indicate an interest in developing "global" strategies. Except for a handful of companies that specifically cite Japan as a strong competitor, most of the other 48 that mentioned international competition say that they are becoming increasingly aware of this issue and are beginning to place greater emphasis on it in their planning. One steel company ruefully admits: "We have done nothing specific, although this is one major cause of the economic problems we are trying to solve."

Other organizations point out that only some of their units find the international marketplace appropriate for planning. A few, mainly industrial products manufacturers and some food companies, report that they have indeed become more internationally oriented and have developed worldwide strategies to cope with international competition and markets. A few nonmanufacturing companies say they have elected to concentrate on their U.S. activities rather than to adopt an international focus at this time.

Exhibit 1: Profiles of Major Expansion and Development Proposals—A Construction Company

These proposals could include, for example, enlarging facilities; obtaining additional resource leases or permits; redesigning present products; developing a new product, service or process; funding developmental work (inside or outside); acquiring a business, patent license, etc.; replacing or modernizing equipment or plant; entering joint ventures or equity involvements; integrating scope of present businesses—horizontally or vertically; entering a new market with present products or services; entering a present market with new products or services; selling a company, business or assets; or closing down (out) an operation.

To provide credence to your project ideas, please be as specific as possible.

A fundamental criterion in our evaluation of proposed projects is that *we know the business;* particularly the market. A second criterion is near-term *profitability and payback* and *attractive cash flow*. Profits should be assured within 36 months of start-up, payback within 60 months. However, if you have sound knowledge of a business which differs from those in which the company is engaged at present, and you believe it has or could achieve the goals we seek, please suggest it for consideration.

Under "Description and Strategic Significance" indicate how the proposal complements the group's objectives.

Under "Anticipated Competitive Reaction" describe what impact this proposal might have on the strategies of competing firms and what actions they might take. Include comments on any special customer-relations consequences.

If resource requirements or financial details are not known, provide the best estimate at this time.

Date:_____

PROFILE OF MAJOR
EXPANSION OR DEVELOPMENT PROPOSAL

Group:_____

Description and Strategic Significance:

Market Outlook:

Anticipated Competitive Reaction:

Financial Highlights:

	1983	1984	1985	1986	1987	1988
Revenue						
Development Expense						
EBIT						
Net Income						
Capital Expenditures						
Operating Working Cap. (Inc.) Dec.						
Cash Flow from Operations						
Total Invested Capital						
After Tax ROI						

DCF-ROI:_____ Payback (years/months):

Chapter 2

Planning Procedures and Techniques

PLANNING SYSTEMS are only effective if they meet the specific needs or wants of top management, as well as the internal needs of the various business units. Most planners find they must fine-tune the system to make it uniquely suited to their organizations' requirements.

Even older, well-established company planning systems evolve continuously; new methods and techniques are constantly being tried and evaluated. In addition, the new critical issues brought about by changing external forces must be factored into development of plans.

Virtually all of the companies participating in this survey have made adjustments in their planning procedures and techniques in their quest for increased effectiveness. (See Table 1.) But even beyond this, a note of flexibility has been introduced in many parts of the planning process in many companies. The original, structured approach of most planning systems seems to be giving way to an easier, adaptive attitude that more truly meets the perceived needs of the organization as a whole. The planner for one company typically comments: "There is less fascination with abstract techniques and more concern with managing the business by focusing on fundamentals."

The planner of a food services firm summarizes the changes made thus: "Less activity, more thinking; less form, more substance; less medium, more message."

Time Horizon

Most companies typically plan on a five-year time horizon, but the turbulent environment has brought the realism of forecasts for this length of time into question. Some 99 companies have changed the time frame for their strategic plans, but the changes reported are not conclusive: Almost as many lengthened their time horizons as shortened them, and some did both during the past five years.

Most of those who have opted for a longer horizon were not using the most common time frame of five years, and added two years to the existing three being used. A few noted that they had gone from one to three years. Among the companies that chose to shorten the planning horizon, most reduced their five-year outlook to three. The exceptions are largely utilities that generally plan on a much longer planning-time horizon. Several went from ten to five years.

More important is the fact that, regardless of the length of time encompassed, many of the companies have chosen to focus on the near term, and pay less attention to the furthest reaches of the time span. Notes one planner: "Emphasis on the near term (three years) helps to relate to budget and P&L performance, but pushes long-range thinking very much into the background."

Other companies have adopted an even more flexible approach: They claim that the same time frame is not appropriate for all their businesses, and that the nature of the business should dictate the period selected. As the planner

Table 1: Changes in Planning Forms and Procedures, 213 Companies[1]

Changes in past five years	Manufacturing Companies Number	Percent	Non-manufacturing Companies Number	Percent	Total Companies Number	Percent
Prescribed formats ...	89	75	65	69	154	72
Planning calendar	65	55	53	56	118	55
Use of competitive intelligence	63	53	38	40	101	47
Use of computer models............	55	46	46	49	101	47
Planning time horizon	51	43	48	51	99	46
Requirements on presentations	56	47	37	39	93	44
Requirements on space or number of pages	58	49	34	36	92	43
Number of strategic reviews	49	41	39	41	88	41
Executive level of strategic reviews ...	42	35	32	34	74	35
Requirements for monitoring the plan	39	33	32	34	71	33
Use of portfolio-management approach	42	35	20	21	62	29
Planning for international units	37	31	11	12	48	22
Other	23	19	21	22	44	21

[1] One company did not report this information.

> **An Industrial Products Company's Credo**
>
> There are some fundamental tenets on which the foregoing ground rules and a successful effort will rest. It is appropriate to spell them out so that they may be agreed upon or discussed in the context of the firm. These basic premises are:
>
> 1. Professional planners may facilitate a planning process, but they do not do the organization's planning.
>
> 2. Strategy development and planning must be performed by the managers who are ultimately responsible for the implementation of the plans.
>
> 3. Creative strategic planning is inherently a group activity and it will involve many different parts of the organization and many different levels of expertise.
>
> 4. Effective strategy management requires more than numerical extrapolations of trends; it involves largely the selection of missions, objectives and strategic alternatives.
>
> 5. The planning process must provide for the development of relevant data bases, qualitative as well as quantitative, that facilitate the development of environmental forecasts, competitive analyses, and the evaluation of strategic alternatives.
>
> 6. The chief executive's responsibility for developing future organizational strategy will center around the development and support of a "strategic management culture" in the organization.
>
> 7. In a strategic management process, questions may be more important than answers. Strategic questions should be asked by managers to foster awareness of options and probable consequences. In the simplest treatment, a manager should specify a mainline scenario, and specify how deviations will be recognized and what the chief implications are if other than that mainline scenario occurs.
>
> 8. This type of process requires dialogue (as contrasted to filling out forms). Such dialogue needs to focus on opportunities, threats, strengths, limitations, competitive posture and, foremost, on those critical factors that make for success or failure. Dialogue emphasizes issues rather than numbers. A strategy statement should not degenerate into a hurriedly assembled preamble to next year's budget.
>
> 9. Finally, strategy and planning efforts must be linked firmly to other systems for allocating and committing capital funds. Capital allocation and subsequent authorization to spend offer the most tangible means for strategic management and controlling decisions of long-term impact. It is through capital or resource allocation that strategic priorities find practical expression.

for a high-technology corporation says: "We dropped the pretense of valid ten-year positions for most business units." An oil company reports that, over the past five years, it "both shortened and lengthened the planning horizon, depending on yearly needs and economic conditions."

Planning Calendar

Some organizations change their planning calendars annually as a matter of course, or as a function of the issues and needs of the company. A number are still experimenting with the most effective timing cycle to suit the needs of their managements.

The changes made in the planning calendar, reported by 118 of the participating companies, reflect principally an attempt to separate the strategic planning and budgeting phases of the planning cycle, or to link strategic plans with operational plans. Many of the companies that made this kind of change wanted the longer-term strategic plan to be developed and reviewed before consideration of the numbers needed for the budget. Rearranging the calendar to allow ample time to elapse between these two phases, many believe, focuses appropriate attention on each. Yet the need to bond the shorter-range operating plans with the strategic plan frequently requires other delicate readjustments in scheduling. The goal of balancing all these requirements is to ensure implementation of the plans.

Other calendar changes were made to fit better with the internal needs of the organization, for example, the needs of the operating units. And, in a few cases, a change in the fiscal year triggered a new planning calendar.

The new flexibility that has entered many company planning systems extends to the planning calendar as well. Several planners report a staggered system of plan submission, with plans coming in from the business units at different times during the year. Some state that planning is now a year-round process in the company, as opposed to "a three-month crunch," in the words of one respondent.

The planner for an industrial products manufacturer claims that the change it made in its planning calendar made

Exhibit 2: Timetable for Strategic Plans—An Information Services Corporation

		1983
1.	Operating units meet with corporate planning staff to review strategic issues and market definitions.	January/February
2.	Operating units submit draft strategic plans to corporate planning department.	May 2nd
3.	Operating units review plans with EVPs, and corporate planning and financial staffs.	May-June
4.	Operating units review plans with CEO and COO as necessary.	June-July
5.	Corporate office issues plan-review letters to operating units.	August
6.	Corporate and selected operating units present strategic plans to the Policy & Planning Committee.	October
7.	The Policy & Planning Committee reports to the Board of Directors.	November

Exhibit 3: Planning Calendar—An Industrial Products Company

2/1-4/15	Situation analysis prepared for each division. Corporate Development and Planning will hold one half-day training session with division marketing personnel in February.
3/16-3/17	Policy Committee meetings with each Division General Manager to discuss the division mission statement, objectives and issues. This meeting is informal. Material does not have to be submitted in advance.
4/18-5/20	Draft division plans prepared. Plans submitted to Corporate.
5/23-6/10	Initial review of plans by Corporate.
6/13-7/5	Plans revised as necessary.
7/6	Plans submitted to the Policy Committee, the Controller, and Corporate Development and Planning.
Week of 7/18	Presentation to the Policy Committee by Division Management.
August-November	Final strategic plans prepared along with the three-year financial plan, operating plans, and budget. Instructions and a timetable will be published in August.
11/30	Highlights of the 1984-1986 Plan and Budget sent to the Board of Directors.
12/13	Division General Manager and Corporate presentations to the Board of Directors.

planning an ongoing activity that provides a logical approach to strategy development. This does not necessarily indicate a trend, however, inasmuch as other companies report the opposite stance: Planning takes place at a specific designated time, as opposed to "all over the calendar."

Some planning timetables and schedules are illustrated in Exhibits 2 to 4. They reflect the highlights of the various company planning cycles.

Strategic Presentations and Reviews

Another planning procedure that shows considerable evidence of change is the nature and composition of the presentations and review meetings. More discussion and informal dialogue are replacing the "dog and pony shows" of yesteryear, according to a number of the planning executives commenting on this point.

The majority of these planners state that there is now an emphasis on establishing dialogue and "real" two-way communication at these events. A question-and-answer format has superseded the polished presentations that formerly marked this phase of the planning process. Even as higher-level executives are now being involved, the meetings are less formal, more interactive, and more focused on issues and strategies. "There is less articulation of documents and more discussion of conclusions, implications, ramifications and reasonableness of the plans," a high-technology com-

Exhibit 4: Planning Process—A Forest Products and Paper Corporation

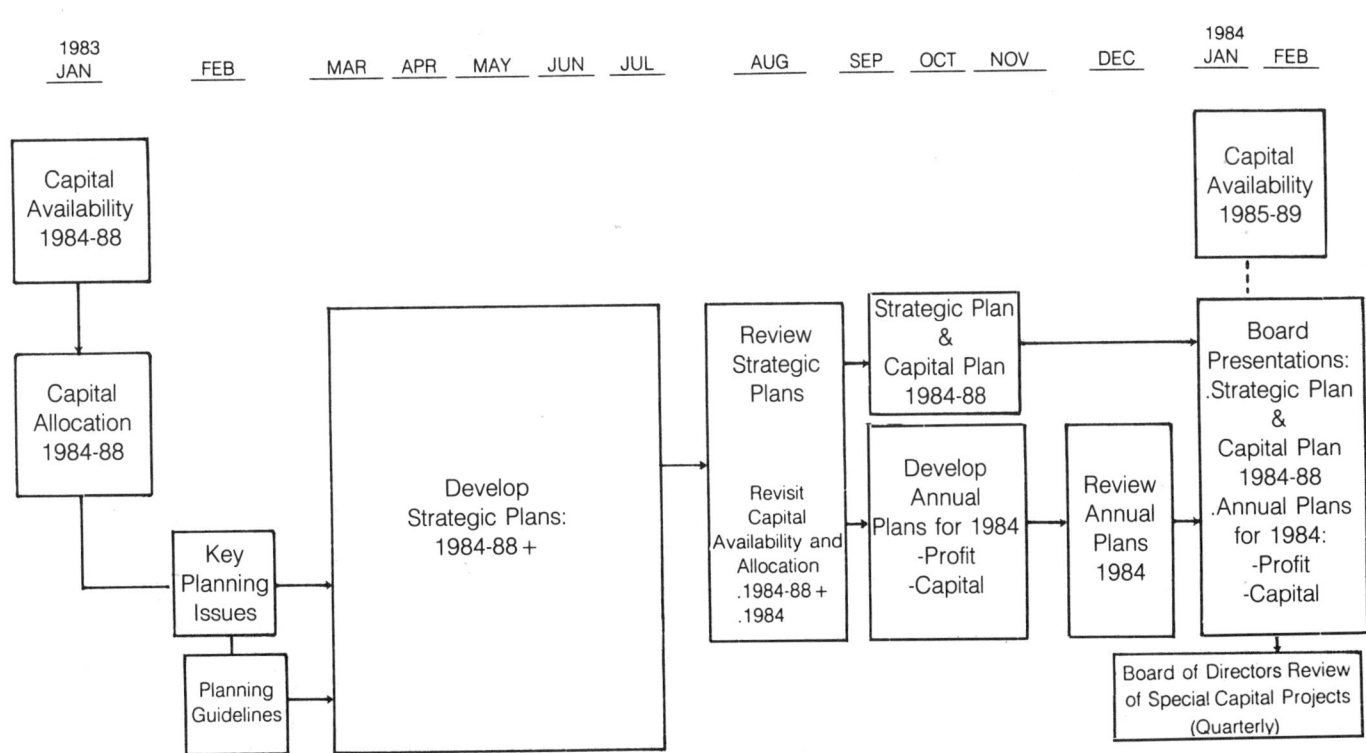

PLANNING PROCEDURES AND TECHNIQUES 7

pany's planner states. "Strategic reviews provide a good forum for the exchange of ideas and information about strategic issues facing the divisions and the company," claims the head of planning of a retail chain.

Reaffirming this shift in emphasis, presentations and reviews focuses on issues, objectives and strategies, rather than on financial data, in many of the reporting companies. Nevertheless, all structure has not been abandoned. In order to utilize the meeting time more efficiently, most planners issue specific requirements for the scheduled presentations to be made to management. They may include statements of the most significant aspects of the plan, such as direction, objectives and major strategies. Supporting data underlying these decisions are frequently asked for as well, but top-level meetings rarely discuss much of this detail.

The guidelines for the preparation and presentation for business-unit strategy meetings in a diversified manufacturing organization include the following instructions:

"Each operation's general manager, general sales and production managers will review with the president's office the mission, phase of strategy, and strategic directions each major business unit intends to follow during the current planning period.

"The purpose of these meetings is a realistic discussion of the various elements affecting the strategic alternatives of each business unit and an agreement on the objectives that will serve as the basis for preparation of a comprehensive plan for the planning period.

"It is suggested that managers concentrate their preparation and presentation in six major areas—(1) historical perspective, (2) business-unit mission and phase of strategy, (3) strengths and weaknesses analysis, (4) new product analysis, (5) critical issues analysis, and (6) overall strategy, objectives and prime strategic actions."

Each of the six categories is further defined and followed by guidelines for the preparation needed, which is used as the basis for discussion. (See Exhibit 5.)

Most companies (such as the publishing firm in Exhibit 6) try to put plan summaries, at least, in the hands of the reviewing members prior to the meeting in order to familiarize them sufficiently to promote knowledgeable discussion. Some planning guidelines also cite post-meeting

Exhibit 5: Major Areas to Be Covered in Plan Presentations—A Diversified Manufacturer

1. The historical perspective based on where each unit's position has been during the past six years, '77-'82, and what its position is today. Using the 1983 Strategic Planning Summary as a guide for discussion, managers should present the following information:
   - Industry definition, size and estimated BU share.
   - Served market definition, estimated size in units and dollars, characteristics, estimated market rank, and estimated market share of BU and top competitors.
   - Business unit's sales dollars and units, operating contribution percentage, ROA, total and current assets, and asset turnover history for the past six years, '77-'82, and approved sales and profit budget for '83. Financial background data for these meetings will be *limited only to historical data* which will be sufficient to provide a perspective for discussion purposes.
   - Compounded annual rates of growth, least-squares method, of the served market sales dollars, BU sales dollars, and sales units compared with Gross National Product or Gross Domestic Product for period '77-'82.

2. Mission Statement and Phase of Strategy—The mission establishes the overall framework within which the BU develops and implements its strategy. The elements included are detailed in the five steps of BU planning.

   The phases of strategy have been renamed and redefined, this year. Managers should use the attached "Business Unit Phases of Strategy" to assist them in determining the appropriate phase. [See Exhibit 10.]

3. Strengths and Weaknesses Analysis will highlight key profit determinants as they impact on the BU As a basis for discussion, managers should use "Guidelines for Preparing Analysis of Strengths and Weaknesses."

4. New Product Analysis will highlight the use of new products in the BU's strategy.

5. Critical Issue Analysis details those few major items which the BU must resolve in order to achieve its objectives.

6. The overall strategy and objectives for the business unit during the planning period. Again, using the 1983 Strategic Planning Summary as a guide, managers should present the following information:
   - Estimates of compounded annual growth rates for served market sales, BU sales dollars, and BU sales units, compared with Gross National Product or Gross Domestic Product for the period '82-'87.
   - Objectives for served market share, operating contribution percentage, asset turnover, and return on assets. Indicate the *specific year for achievement for each of the four objectives.*
   - The prime strategic actions relating to product and marketing; research and development and styling; and fixed and current assets that will be undertaken to implement the strategy.

Exhibit 6: Instructions for Preparation for Plan Review Meetings—A Newspaper Publisher

Planning review meetings will be held with individual companies for the purpose of presenting and evaluating five-year plans and forecasts. A preliminary schedule for these meetings is included in the package. In order to facilitate informed discussion at these meetings, it is requested that each company president submit a draft plan and financial forecast to the group vice president (one copy), and vice president of planning and development (nine copies) *at least two weeks prior to the date of the company review* for distribution to other corporate participants. The meetings then serve as a forum for constructive discussion of business plans among subsidiary, group and corporate personnel.

The senior group vice president will chair the planning review, but each company president should arrange a presentation. The agenda may vary among companies, but should be structured to summarize, in succinct fashion, the following areas of interest:

1. Review of accomplishments and progress against budgets and plans in the current year.
2. Discussion of significant changes (e.g., revisions and updating) in each element of the prior business plan (i.e., market outlook, company position, objectives and goals, and operational and development plan).
3. Review of financial forecasts.

The meetings are scheduled to last approximately two to three hours.

Each company president should decide who will participate from his organization. It is suggested that attendees be limited to key personnel who are directly and importantly concerned with the development, implementation or application of the plans and forecasts under review. (Other company personnel requiring this information can be provided with copies of the final plan.) On the corporate side the group vice presidents, vice president of planning and development, and other appropriate finance and accounting representatives will attend every meeting. Other corporate management or staff may be invited for special purposes, although it is desired that attendance be limited to key personnel in order to encourage an open exchange of opinion on management programs.

---

requirements. The publishing company, for example, issues these instructions:

"Following the review meeting, plans and forecasts may be revised or modified according to instructions of the group vice president, and then resubmitted in final form for consolidation. To facilitate review and processing of such changes, *only revised pages* of plans and forecasts should be resubmitted at this time. Such revisions are due within two weeks after the review meetings."

And a food company's instructions note: "Questions will undoubtedly be raised during the presentation, and not all of them will be resolved at that time. A representative of the business unit or division should record those questions that are not answered. A written response to these should be issued within one week."

In general, the choice of attendees at these meetings has become more selective, with an emphasis on raising the level of those present. Most of the surveyed companies, as a matter of fact, stress that review committees or attendees are now top and senior managers, and that only the necessary principals involved are in the room at meetings.

Another sign of the new flexibility entering the planning process in many companies is that many strategic reviews are held irregularly, when needed, or only for selected businesses. For example, a diversified corporation's planner says that the company is "moving from reviews of every strategic business unit with the chief executive to reviews of high impact and new businesses." Others review problem units more frequently. Several respondents mention that strategic reviews are called when issues of strategic importance surface, or as the business environment warrants.

Informality and dialogue may mean shorter, pithier meetings, but not necessarily fewer meetings. In fact, more companies report having increased the number of their strategic reviews than say they have reduced the number of such regularly scheduled meetings.

Competitive Intelligence

The use of competitive intelligence, competitor analysis, and new techniques for gaining a competitive edge has been a major factor in developing strategies over the past five years, according to the survey results. This is exemplified by a large insurance company's planning director, who remarks: "We now watch with varying degrees of interest about 200 competitors, most of which were never considered competitors four years ago. We used to watch about five companies."

Of the 101 companies that have changed their competitive intelligence procedures or planning formats over the last five years, almost all now place increased emphasis on monitoring, analyzing and evaluating their competitors and their specific industry environments. While some maintain an informal, subjective approach to the competition, others have initiated more comprehensive, intensive and integrated methods and procedures. (A few companies report they have increased the use of consultants to help in gathering competitive data.)

Several companies say they have delegated the responsibility for monitoring the competition to the business units from its former center in the corporate planning department. Although operating units are usually good sources of competitive information, they may not be familiar with analytic techniques for interpreting data. Many planning guidelines, therefore, provide instructions, examples and a general discussion on competitive analysis to guide managers through this part of the planning exercise. An industrial products company, for instance, explains the context for competitive analysis as follows:

"For most businesses, the key to success or failure of future strategies lies with the competitors and what they can and will do. Given this basic fact, it is remarkable how seldom companies focus on the personalities and capabilities of the competitors that they face.

"Our premise should be that companies' competitors are knowable. The quality of that knowledge must of necessity be somewhat less precise than companies are used to in dealing with their own internal data. What is wanted is not accounting accuracy, but a big-picture evaluation of what a competitor is *able* to do (his strengths and weaknesses) and what he is *likely* to do (his personality). The objective is to use these data to build a profile which has a high probability of being directionally accurate. Business is, after all, a game of odds, and over time a company that assesses its competitors as carefully as possible is likely to do better than one which does not.

"Frequently, companies and businesses possess isolated qualitative data about their competitors. The quantity of such data is often great, particularly when one aggregates or collects all the information known by all the employees.

"It is astounding what plant managers, salesmen, new hires in R&D, etc., know about the competitors a company is facing. The problems with this information are that it is fragmented and that the perspective is limited, usually relating only to those businesses with direct competitive interface. And, of course, the competitors' businesses may include many in which the client does not compete.

"The result is that *most companies feel they do not need any more analysis about their competitors, because they already know so much; but in fact, they are unable to use what they do know in a meaningful way.* Thus, it is not at all uncommon for individual businesses to fail to exploit opportunities which have been presented by competitors who are either incapable or unwilling to be as aggressive as they might be. Similarly, it is not unusual to find businesses which consistently propose plans which, given the strength of competition, are clearly attempting to fight the law of competitive gravity.

"What is needed is a way to structure information about competitors, to purposefully oversimplify a competitor's position in order to create a big-picture framework around which to organize all that is known about each competitor."

It concludes: "Clearly more art than science, competitive analysis is a dynamic process. It is even more dynamic than the strategy formulation that is so dependent upon an appreciation of competitors and competitive response. An attempt to produce a structured document that routinely describes probable competitive actions and reactions is not likely to be successful. What is required is a sense of getting into the competitor's mind and anticipating his moves. One effective way of accomplishing this is the designation of an individual, on a collateral duty basis, to be the focal point for all data and analysis and resultant information on a given competitor."

The questions that should be examined for each competitor, according to the planning guides of an industrial products company are:

"What is the current strategy?"
"What is the future strategy likely to be?"
"What are strengths, resources and weaknesses?"
"How has the competitor reacted to competitive moves in the past?"
"Where is the competitor most—and least—vulnerable?"
"Where are we most—and least—vulnerable to each competitor?"

This firm also asks, for the three largest competitors, for an evaluation of their product and market, current strategy, strengths, weaknesses, likely future strategy, and other relevant information. This is in addition to an examination of their historic market share and projected market share.

A diversified manufacturer also asks its managers to consider and comment on the strengths and weaknesses and perceived strategies of its three principal competitors. It breaks down the major characteristics as follows:

1. Market effectiveness
   Sales force
   Distribution
   Product line
   Product quality
   Perceived product pricing
   Merchandising and advertising
   Production mix

2. Technological effectiveness
   Product styling and design
   Patents or exclusive products
   Capacities and capacity utilization
   Technological breakthroughs
   R&D effort

3. Cost effectiveness
   Perceived profitability
   Perceived financial strength
   Perceived manufacturing costs—low cost producer in industry?
   Other expenses—comparison with business unit and competitors?

An industrial products company has developed a form to express its position in the competitive environment of its particular industry. It supplies explicit instructions for filling out the form. (See Exhibit 7.) And a food products

Exhibit 7: Instructions for Competitive Environment Analysis—An Industrial Equipment Manufacturer

The intent of this form is to express how well the company is positioned within this particular industry.

Market Share Profile

If the column titles are inappropriate, change them in a way which will provide an understanding of competitive market shares.

Competitive Strategies

List the key competitors and describe their strengths and strategies.

<u>Distinctive Competence</u>—Predominant strength of competitor which is unique in the industry—should be *functional* and not a market segment. What is competitor really good at doing?

<u>Segment Strength</u>—Strongest current segment of competitor; could be geographic, application or customer type.

<u>Strategy</u>—The following is a list of typical strategies which might be appropriate to describe either the company's or a competitor's strategy.

Applications—Emphasizing specific applications. (Identify)

Demand Creation—Changing primary customer awareness and desire to use product—stimulating primary demand.

Pricing—Raising, holding or lowering prices, terms conditions or financing. Although all strategies involve pricing policies, a pricing thrust implies a strategy strictly based on price terms— e.g., a penetration based on low prices. (Identify any key segments)

Distribution—Expanding, holding or contracting how and where product is sold.

Segment Emphasis—Geographic or market segment emphasis. (Identify segment)

Service—Increasing or decreasing support services.

Capacity—Increasing or decreasing capacity or its utilization—e.g., add capacity in new or existing regions to improve market share. (Identify regions) Involves decisions on whether capacity leads, lags or matches demand.

Process Innovation—Increasing market size or penetration by process innovation.

Supply and Sourcing—Changing relative dependence on suppliers of materials—e.g., backward integration.

Revolution—Creating an entirely new market through new breakthroughs.

Evolution—Adding new capabilities to product line.

Differentiation—Changing perceived characteristics or product.

Company Vulnerabilities

List the vulnerabilities of this business to each of the areas identified. Briefly describe the threat and estimate the percentage of the business which is vulnerable. It may be appropriate to add a category (e.g., governmental budget or regulation) or to substitute for a category.

COMPETITIVE ENVIRONMENT

MARKET SHARE PROFILE			
COMPETITOR	CAPACITY	CAPACITY SHARE	MARKET SHARE

COMPETITIVE STRATEGIES			
COMPETITOR	DISTINCTIVE COMPETENCE	SEGMENT STRENGTH	STRATEGY
[Company]			

(continued)

Exhibit 7: Instructions for Competitive Environment Analysis—An Industrial Equipment Manufacturer (continued)

[Company] VULNERABILITIES TO:	BRIEF DESCRIPTION	% OF BUSINESS VULNERABLE
SUBSTITUTE PRODUCTS	EXAMPLES VSA—Substitute for LIN in high purity *gas* application.	X% of IGD sales
CUSTOMER(S)	X number of customer steel mills have old technology vulnerable to shutdown.	X% of metallurgical sales
SUPPLIER(S)	New Orleans CO_2 business vulnerable to continued viability of NH_3 plant.	X% of business vulnerable
COMPETITOR(S)	Chang Chung PVOH pricing policies.	lower overall pricing
ENERGY PRICING		

company asks for an analysis of each of its competitors on a one-page form. (See Exhibit 8.)

Even beyond the broader search for more information on competitors, some companies are searching for a broader *definition* of their competition. Recent upheavals have confronted companies in several industries with a whole new set of different, or potential, competitors.

Several planners point out that competitive intelligence is an area in which they are relatively weak and are working toward improvement. In a transportation company that has put emphasis on knowing the competition, the planner reports that this effort has "intensified in terms of quality as the subsidiaries come to understand the value of in-depth analysis."

Computers and Computer Models

The use of computers and computer models in the planning process has gained greater acceptance in the past few years, according to the companies surveyed. Only eight of the 101 reporting a change have discontinued the use of a computer model, or use it less than they did previously.

Even among the companies that have introduced this technique only within the past three years, there is already increased usage. Several firms have upgraded their hardware, and others continue to develop new models and more sophisticated uses. Strategic planning, financial forecasting and econometric models are among those mentioned, and planners cite capabilities that will be added shortly. A diversified industrial products company's planner reports that the strategic plan was computerized five years ago; "now the short-term plan is also on the computer, and integrated with the strategic plan."

A financial services firm makes extensive use of simulation modeling, and several utilities report increased usage. One says: "Existing models are used more for strategic analysis. We now use simpler but broader models with

Exhibit 8: Format for Competitive Analysis—A Food Products Company

COMPETITOR ANALYSIS*

OUR PRODUCT LINE:_____

COMPETITOR'S NAME:_____

Market Share
Share Trend
Long-Range Commitments
Expansion Plans
Estimated Priorities
Estimated Objectives
Strengths
Weaknesses
Competitive Advantage
Resources:
   Investment
   Capacity and Utilization
   Marketing Level
   Financial Resources
   Past Success

One Page For Each Competitor

graphics and have added decision analysis and decision-tree capabilities." An oil company's respondent describes its practice: "A model was developed for continual update of financial projections and ratios as new and revised data become available." Another responding company has established competitive simulations to project their top four

FACING STRATEGIC ISSUES: NEW PLANNING GUIDES AND PRACTICES

competitors' P&L's—based on volume trends, cost pressures, and pricing.

Computers models appear to be used primarily for financial analysis, but several firms have found some quick "what-if" type applications. A steel company, for example, explains that it has shifted from cumbersome all-encompassing models toward "more flexible models that give answers to small what-if questions." A number of companies state that there has been significantly increased use of computers for consolidation of plans at the corporate level, in addition to the various types of analyses in which models excel.

To put the use of the computer model in proper perspective, a utility company instructs as well as cautions its managers:

"One of the tools utilized in the analysis of strategic alternatives is the corporate model. The model simulates the major relationships and interactions between each major segment of the company's business and consists of a number of linked computer submodels. It is very important to note that the corporate model is a *tool* to be utilized in the planning process; the *model* is *not* the process. The planner should continue to remind himself of this to avoid inversion of means and ends. The model is a *means* to an end—the end being the analysis of alternatives and development of a strategic plan. If the planner allows himself to get immersed too deeply in the details of the model he can tend to become more concerned with the model itself than with the process. The model is a mechanism to be used to enhance the corporate planning process, not vice versa."

The planner in a high-technology company observes that "there is vast use to verify 'credibility' (equals quality) of numerical plans." He cautions, however, that "it is easy to *overuse.*"

Portfolio Management Approach

Of the more sophisticated planning techniques in use over the past decade, probably none has drawn so much attention from executives and the business press as the portfolio-management approach. Experience with its use has varied considerably over time, the survey shows.

Of the 62 companies reporting changes in their use of the portfolio-management approach to setting strategy, 34 say they have either introduced or increased the use of this technique during the past five years. A diversified company's planner says: "We now use it extensively in reviewing corporate strategy and resetting direction."

Slow acceptance by management, particularly in the operating units, is an apparent drawback to more exten-

---

Exhibit 9: Business Classification Explanations—An Engineering and Construction Firm

Growth: Businesses are classified as "Growth" if they participate in market segments having growth rates greater than GNP and/or if the company's competitive advantages are expected to result in a significant increase in market share.

The strategies for a "Growth" business generally will reflect several of the following characteristics:
— Relates to markets having higher-than-average growth rates.
— Enjoys a clearly identifiable competitive advantage, either existing or potential (e.g., proprietary, market share, service, reputation, design differentiation, etc.)
— High margins and increasing market share are primary management-performance criteria.
— A requirement for substantial additional resources (including management time).
— A tendency to be net cash users during the plan period.

Maintenance: Businesses are classified as "Maintenance" if their primary focus is to maintain existing market share, exploit earnings or cash-flow potential, or continue complementary support of other company businesses.

Maintenance business strategies generally will reflect several of the following characteristics:
— A tendency to be net cash generators during the plan period.
— Relates to markets experiencing GNP growth rates or lower, perhaps even declining markets.
— Cash-flow growth and improved use of working capital are primary management-performance criteria.
— Revenue growth is not a primary management-performance criterion.
— Low-cost producer, market niche, and/or product differentiation are important elements in increasing success.

Divestiture (or Phase Out): These are businesses which are of little future strategic interest to the company and a plan to withdraw is being, or should be, developed.

The strategies for businesses in this category will be oriented toward increasing the attractiveness of spinning off, selling or phasing out. The strategies would typically result in short-term improvements in cash flow and/or earnings as against the results anticipated from other strategies.

Uncertainty: Businesses are placed in this category temporarily because of inability to classify them otherwise, due to such things as changing economic or market conditions, unclear government policy, new competitive environment, and so on. Over time, profit centers or businesses in this category would be identified as Growth, Maintenance, or Divestiture (Phase Out).

Strategies of these business will reflect short-term improvements and a "wait-and-see" attitude with appropriate review benchmarks.

Exhibit 10: Business Unit Phases of Strategy—A Diversified Manufacturer

CHARACTERISTICS	MANAGE FOR:				
	NEW BUSINESS DEVELOPMENT	GROWTH	SUSTAINED EARNINGS	CASH	EXIT
Served Market Growth	Potential for high growth in relation to GNP	High growth in relation to GNP	Approaching GNP	Declining in relation to GNP	Sharply declining in relation to GNP
Market Share Position	Potential to gain rapidly	Gaining rapidly	High	High	Variable
Technology, Manufacturing and Marketing Position	Potential to achieve superior positions	Developing superior positions	Leadership	Mature	Declining
Profitability	Potential to exceed the cost of capital	Growing to exceed the cost of capital	Consistently and significantly exceeds the cost of capital	At or above the cost of capital	Unacceptable
Cash Flow	Negative; in line with development costs	Generally negative; moving toward positive	Strongly positive	Maximum	Unacceptable
RESOURCE SUPPORT	Sufficient to prove the feasibility of each stage in the development process	Maximum in line with desired growth objectives	Focused in areas that will sustain market share, profitability and cash flow	Curtailed to generate maximum cash flow	Minimal

NOTE: In determining a business unit's phase of strategy, the characteristics listed above will normally apply; however, there may be exceptions.

sive use, some respondents claim. A few companies have modified the portfolio-management elements to overcome this initial resistance by managers, and several planners say that the technique is being used more as it becomes better accepted.

To explain the rationale of portfolio-management analysis and the strategic implications to be drawn from it, several planning manuals devote a portion of their guides to describing this technique. Some examples are shown in Exhibits 9 to 11.

Eleven companies, principally manufacturing companies, report they have discontinued the use of this technique or use it selectively. One company focuses less on this now, its spokesman says, because it "was creating unrealistic alternatives." Another claims it is using "a more realistic approach" because, the planner comments, "Dogs are not all bad."

Avoiding Surprise: Forecasts, Assumptions, Scenarios, Contingency Planning

All plans have to be based on some kinds of assumptions about a future that is ultimately unknowable. Many managements have expressed dissatisfaction with their lack of success in forecasting, and it remains a troublesome subject that is receiving increased attention.

It is common for corporate headquarters to issue a broad range of economic and financial assumptions as a means of promoting consistency among the individual plans of its subsidiaries, divisions and other business units. These are usually five-year outlooks for the general economic environment and frequently include such factors as: gross national product, monetary and fiscal environment, capital markets, market trends, production-material costs, and energy prices.

These forecasts may be developed with the help of a corporate economist, or special environmental task forces or units, if they exist in the organization. But they are more commonly derived from the large number of economic and environmental scanning services that sell such data.

An aerospace manufacturer with an active corporate program of environmental scanning explains the relationship between the corporate services and reports provided, and the business units' responsibilities.

"Environmental scanning and assessment is an integral part of the strategic planning process at the company. An understanding of the environment and its impacts on our lines of business is critical to our future success. As a result of its direct impact on a line of business, most environmental scanning is best done at the operating-company levels since only those directly involved can best understand those environmental factors which influence a particular line of business. However, there are many external environment developments which affect many or all of our companies, and the corporation recognizes its responsibility to add value in this important area as well. Besides encouraging environmental scanning and competitor analysis at the

Exhibit 11: Strategic Analysis of Strategic Business Units—A Chemical Company

Two basic dimensions determine priority in allocation of resources—the attractiveness of the industry and the strength of our business within it. In order to have a commonly understood language within the organization, a strategic grid was developed by which SBU's are assigned to a strategic classification (Exhibit A). This will serve as a basic for: (1) the development of appropriate strategies at the SBU level, (2) discussions with corporate management, and (3) a structural analysis of the corporation.

I. Determinants of Classification

The following determinants should be used to arrive at a strategic classification:
- Market Growth
- Technological Position
- Relative Total Cost Position
- Product Integration
- Raw Material Position
- Return on Investment
- Dependence on External Cycles
- Industry Concentration

II. Strategic Classification

We presently distinguish among four major strategic classifications, which can also be identified in Exhibit A.

Strategic Category 1—"Build Market Share—Priority: Growth"

This is comparable to the "star" category. Although no single mold can be developed which fits all businesses, at least several of the following criteria should be met:
- It should be a product line in which the company has a leading or strong position in a large market. In other words, it has a superior market position (market share) and technological position, and belongs to the leading companies in this field.
- The market has a high growth potential compared with the respective industry and our company.
- The products fit into our business, and synergistic effects with other product groups can be expected.
- The return should potentially be above average compared with the corporate and industry average.
- The product is early enough in its product life cycle that business-cycle influences are minimal.

Strategic Category 2—"New Areas of Interest and Areas Requiring Special Review"

This group covers all product lines which are in the process of introduction. It also includes products which are presently not successful but for which we feel an opportunity still exists. Finally, it includes products which are problem areas, have turned around, but continued success still needs to be proven. They are subdivided into two categories:

  A. "Opportunity Areas"
  B. "Strategies Being Tested"

Below are some criteria for this group:
- This strategic category concerns new products or new fields of interest.
- The product or product group is based on patents, know-how, and/or total cost, which provide an advantage over our competition.
- The new field provides the company with an entry into a major part of the market with high growth and earnings potential.
- The current return is not critical. Future returns are expected to be above average.
- The product is early enough in the life cycle that cyclical influences are minimal.

Strategic Category 3 (Also includes older Category 4)—"Maintain Market Share—Priority: Profitability, Positive Cash Flow"

This is comparable to the "cash cow" category and major criteria are:
- Product groups which represent a major share of current sales and are sold to markets with significant competition and cyclical behavior.
- Our position regarding technology, total costs, and raw materials is between satisfactory and good.
- The return corresponds to the corporate average and/or that of our competition.

Strategic Category 5—"Strategic Change Required"

Some of the criteria are:
- Product groups where we have a weak position concerning market share, technology, total costs, and raw materials.
- Market expectations are poor; slow or stagnating growth can be expected.
- The return is unsatisfactory or the business shows a loss.
- Overall, the long-term outlook for the business is poor.

(continued)

Exhibit 11: Strategic Analysis of Strategic Business Units—A Chemical Company (continued)

Exhibit A: BUSINESS UNIT STRATEGIC SUMMARY
PRODUCT GROUP CLASSIFICATION

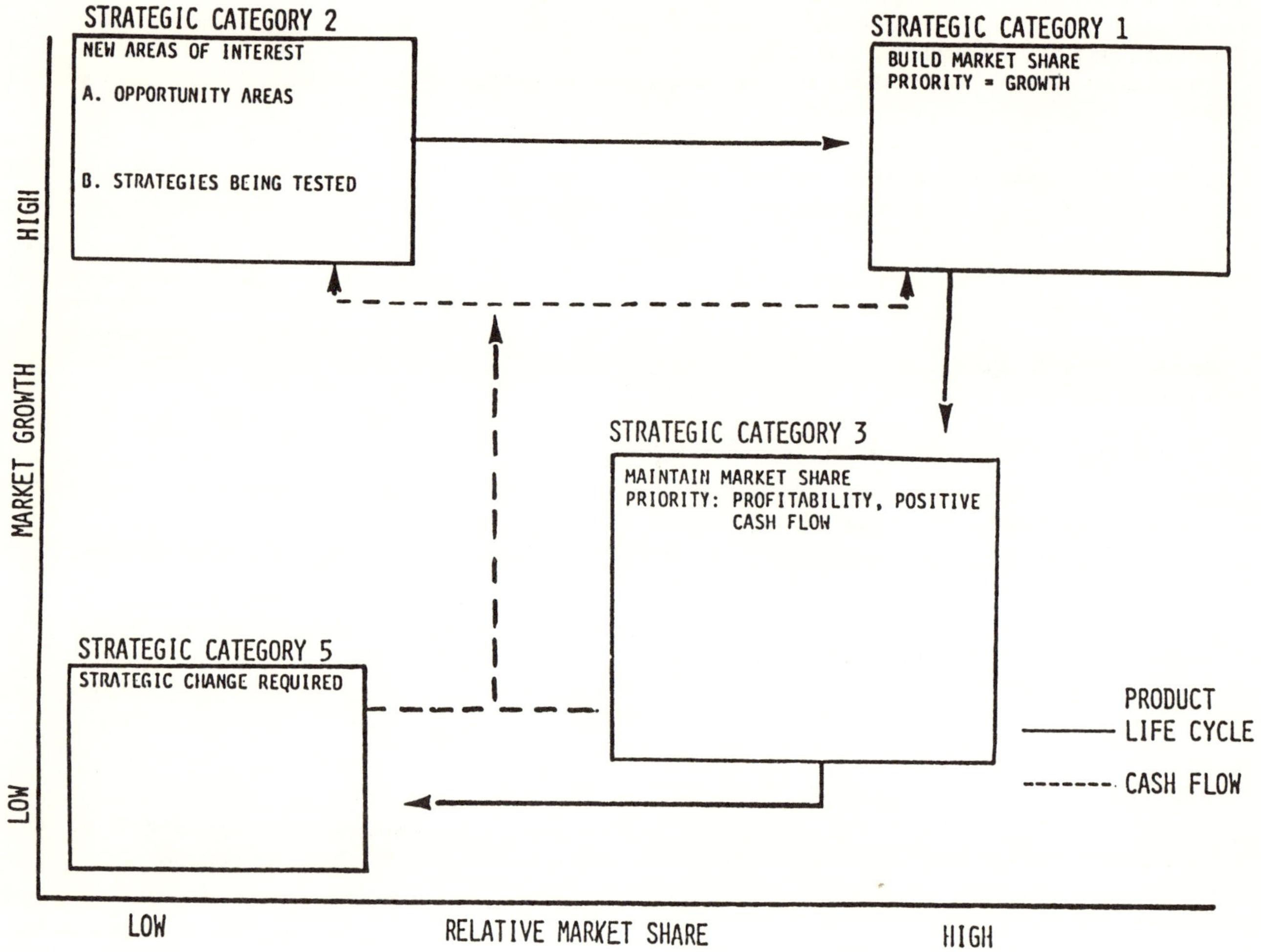

operating company level through the strategic-planning process, the corporation is currently undertaking several activities related to scanning as it relates to corporatewide issues and facilitates the sharing of environmental information. In addition, we encourage the operating companies to come forward with environmental scanning information of a general nature so that this information can be shared throughout the corporation."

One-third of the 214 reporting companies claim that they are making changes in the scope of the assumptions prepared for developing plans. Most of them have broadened the range of the environmental factors they monitor, even though the primary focus remains on economic factors. Here again, industries that are particularly sensitive to specific influences, such as demographic or legislative trends, track those closely. All, however, keep a watchful eye on economic and financial forces that strongly affect their businesses.

But many companies believe a corporatewide view of the environment is not enough. These managements require that the business units themselves must assess and evaluate factors that are critical to the particular business. They call for the unit managers to supply certain assumptions and forecasts as part of their planning requirements. (See Exhibit 12.) A chemical firm, for example, advises its managers to identify those factors "most critical to attaining the forecast performance." They should be "truly pivotal events or significant roadblocks to achievement." This is important, the guide points out, "because it rounds out the premises on which the plan *and its acceptability* are based."

An insurance company explains three advantages in defining assumptions to its managers:

"1. Before corporate management can approve your plan, it must know that you have considered the outside

Exhibit 12: Instructions for Environmental Assumptions—An Industrial Products Company

While broad economic forecasts may be generated on a corporatewide basis, the business manager is most knowledgeable about specific market activities and industry trends. He is best able to assess available information, make preliminary judgments as to relevance, and ultimately develop a list of the most pertinent social, political, technological, economic and competitive conditions likely to underlie future operations. The environmental assumptions should be trends that are very fundamental and very durable, ones that will continue to affect a business significantly for some time to come. If a high inflation rate persists, given that inflation how can you make a profit?

The narrative might be framed in the form of answers to the following questions: What major (not more than five) environmental assumptions will have an impact on our business in the future? In the form of an integrated scenario, how will they affect:

(a) Markets and market segments,
(b) Competition and industry structure,
(c) Fundamental cost structures in the business,
(d) The structure and source of supply of key raw materials?

No one has facts about the future; and though management may seek help from economists, sociologists, futurologists, and the like, management itself must do the disciplined, integrated thinking in deducing the evolving patterns of markets, competition and cost. The purpose is not to forecast events right on the nose; it is to develop a number of strategic alternatives against the one for our key competitors and deduce which environmental assumption is the key. Then, how can we monitor it; or more, how can we influence it?

---

environment as a whole, and more specifically your own relation to it.

"2. In evaluating your plans, corporate management must be aware of the premises upon which the plans are based.

"3. Plans should be changed to meet changing conditions; defining the key assumptions underlying the plan helps alert everyone concerned to the kinds of changes in external conditions that might require changes in plans."

A diversified manufacturing corporation tries to simplify and structure the task of assessment by asking its managers to select from a checklist supplied by corporate headquarters the most significant and relevant assumptions affecting the business climate for the industry, the behavior of the industry, the market, and outside influences such as government regulations and social or political changes. The guide notes that managers are not to list economic and energy assumptions that are substantially the same as those provided by corporate headquarters. This is the checklist supplied:

- "Economy
    —degree of government influence
    —competitive climate
- "Industry
    —growth
    —stability
    —competitor actions
    —growth of markets from which demand is derived
    —potential threats (e.g., technological obsolescence)
    —price trends
    —cost trends (including labor)
- "Market
    —price trends (by market)
    —growth trends
- "Outside influences

    —corporate or group pressures (e.g., impact of previous and present corporate strategy)
    —labor climate
    —social trends (e.g., consumerism, equal opportunity)
    —government."

Other companies that list the kinds of factors to be considered ask for an estimation of the impact of trends in their relevant industry areas. A pharmaceuticals firm, for example, cites:

- "Patent protection and expiration
- "Human resources
- "Technology developments and breakthroughs
- "Availability and cost of materials, supplies and energy
- "Legislative, regulatory, political expectations
- "Cost and price influences
- "Market growth and direction
- "Distribution patterns
- "Consumer influence
- "Competitive developments
- "Etc."

The difficulties of generating realistic forecasts and assumptions have popularized another development over the past five years: the increased use of alternative scenarios in the planning process. Several companies have adopted multiscenario planning to prepare for uncertainty in the future, particularly when they believe that the base case formulated may be optimistic.[1]

An oil company cites four objectives in using scenarios:

"1. Assess the environmental risk associated with the plan update,

---

[1] For a discussion of the use of scenarios in planning, see Rochelle O'Connor, *Planning Under Uncertainty*. The Conference Board, Report 741, 1978.

Examining Alternate Views of the Future

Alternate scenarios were introduced recently in an industrial products company's planning guide with this explanation:

"The 1970's have taught us to be very wary of forecasts. The techniques of forecasting are, in general, premised on the belief that the future is a product of the past, and that future trends and events are somehow related to past trends and events. If this were the case, strategic planning would be a meaningless concept. On the contrary, we have seen that the world is changing with alarming rapidity and that the past is not a very good guide to the future. In this world of rapid change and uncertainty, effective strategic planning is becoming a critical factor in corporate decision making.

"The ultimate concern of the strategic-planning effort is to support this decision-making process. But how can one make decisions affecting the long-range future of the corporation in an environment of rapid change and uncertainty? The so-called "Expected Case" has proven to be of little value in planning. We are continuously surprised by the unexpected turn of events and frustrated when our well-conceived plans have to be abandoned.

"Earlier this year, when we were discussing the broad outlines of the Year-2000 Project, we settled upon two objectives:

"The development of procedures and techniques to help us understand the implications of change and the uncertainty to the company.

"The preparation of long-range strategies which recognize this highly uncertain future environment.

Not surprisingly, we have not figured out how to eliminate the uncertainty. We can't predict the future. We never could and we never will. We do believe, however, that we can effectively do something about the element of surprise by examining the implications to our businesses of different future developments. These alternate views of the future are described as scenarios.

What Are Scenarios Anyway?

"First of all, scenarios are not forecasts. There are an infinite number of possible future outcomes and paths to achieve these outcomes. A scenario is a coherent, internally consistent, and credible set of economic and social circumstances that could emerge from our present environment. We will be presenting later three scenarios which describe separate and distinct views of the future, versions of which have been discussed at length in the press this year. The likelihood that any one of them will occur exactly as stated is small. We have tried to develop three scenarios that represent what we might think of as three different boundary conditions, recognizing that what actually occurs could be some combination of all three, or altogether different.

"The primary purpose of the scenarios is to provide a tool for focusing on and analyzing the company's vulnerability and opportunities under distinctly different sets of external environments. The major benefit of the proper use of scenarios is that the various aspects of a business will be thought through under a different set of environmental factors. If the scenarios have been properly selected, major issues of concern to our businesses will be identified and discussed and the element of surprise should be greatly diminished. Had we used scenarios in the late 1970's, the consequences of the rapid increase and subsequent decline in petroleum prices on the synfuels and petroleum industries could have been anticipated. We may not have made any decision differently, but we probably would not have been surprised by the turn of events.

"Elimination of surprise is, then, our first goal. Formulation of strategies that explicitly recognize the possibility of alternate futures, is the second."

The discussion goes on to point out that the scenarios provided are "for background for thinking about your business." The shorter-term scenarios will be used "as the backbone for your plan, as in the past. The longer-term scenarios . . . are intended as background against which to analyze the key assumptions and risk in your plan. . . . We are not looking for multiple plans. We want one plan with an assessment of your major assumptions and what the impact on your plan would be if your assumption is wrong and something else does occurs. In other words, where are the risks—both upside and downside?"

"2. Improve the corporation's understanding of how external variables influence performance,

"3. Provide the senior executive with range projections of corporate performance, and

"4. Help select environmentally robust strategies."

Managers in a large food company, who had been asked to test their plans against a high-inflation and low-growth scenario in one year, were asked to test them the following year against low inflation rates and low growth "to see what impact might be expected under these circumstances."

Further to avoid surprise, a number of companies have put more emphasis on developing contingency plans. For the most part, this exercise has been introduced somewhat cautiously. Most of the companies with requirements for contingency planning stress that the identification of possible critical events and their impact, rather than a full set of alternate plans, is the principal objective of this requirement.[2]

"Corporate management is mindful of the fact that contingency planning not only takes a great deal of time," states the planning guide of a food company, "but also runs the risk of diverting management's attention from its principal planning job. Therefore, corporate management feels that contingency planning should be kept simple and limited to major issues; not a detailed or full-blown replanning exercise. Our corporate contingency-planning process has seldom resulted in numerous alternatives, but rather has

[2] See the discussion in O'Connor, 1978, pp. 13-26.

Exhibit 13: Contingency Plans Instructions—An Industrial Products Manufacturer

PLANNING GUIDELINES	NOTES
Under "Environmental Assessment" several long-term key high-impact variables were identified. Pick the two that you think are most likely to occur. Then: 　For their pessimistic values, state what you would do (contingency plan) and when (trigger point). 　For their optimistic values, do the same. 　　　　　　　　　　　　　　　　　　　　　*Examples follow*	

_____ CONTINGENCY PLANS _____

KEY CONTINGENT EVENTS	TRIGGER POINTS	CONTINGENCY PLANS
Large increase in natural gas and oil prices	$ /unit	Convert boilers to coal.
Current chrome-plating supplier discontinues operations	First notification of suppliers intent to discontinue operations	Buy or build chrome-plating facility for Youngstown operations.
Current supplier of brass parts continues to sell to "pirates"	Supplier still selling to "pirates" by April 1, 1983	Begin production of brass parts.

Exhibit 14: Contingency Planning Instructions—An Insurance Firm

Standard Procedure

　The purpose of contingency planning is to develop alternative strategies and possibly to revise goals in order to prepare for the occurrence of an event that could have significant impact on the conduct of your future business.

　In *1980*, each unit undertook contingency planning for the special issues of accelerating inflation and an energy crisis. In addition, some units prepared contingency plans on other issues of special importance to them.

　Contingency planning is "What If" planning. It is an outgrowth of your environmental analysis. In analyzing your environment, you may identify events which, if they occur, could be very disruptive to the conduct of your business and your plans in the future. These events may be opportunities as well as threats. Your best judgment at this time may be that they will not occur. However, if they do occur, your existing strategies and your plan may not account for their effects. These major disruptions could present great opportunity to those who are prepared and able to capitalize on the event in a timely and efficient manner. Or, they could have major adverse effects if we are not ready to minimize their impact.

　It is important to plan for the possibility of disruptions—to assess their impact and to outline strategies and programs to meet them. In essence, the company wants to have on the shelf a series of contingency plans to meet critical issues—both to take advantage of the opportunities offered and minimize the effect of any calamity.

　A contingency plan consists of a narrative paper—no more than three to five pages in length. It is not a completely detailed strategic plan for each issue. All that is needed is a brief discussion of the anticipated impacts of the issue on your operation and the revised strategies required to take advantage of—or to cope with—the situation. A broad indication of the changes in expected revenues and profits should be given, but a complete numerical financial plan is not required. The contingency plan should focus on new markets and new products, or changes in procedures, systems and expenses to take advantage of, or to counter, disruptive change.

　This year, as last, each unit is asked to develop a list of the important events or issues for which a contingency plan should be useful. This is a list of the major events or issues that could affect the achievement of your plan. This information will give the Strategic Planning Committee a broad, overall look at the *major* threats and opportunities facing the total company today and it will summarize the "threats" (positive or negative) to your plan. You do not have to develop a contingency plan for each of these events or issues, but only to present a list of those which warrant contingency plans in the future.

　If there are issues for which you feel a contingency plan should be developed *this year,* you are encouraged to develop that contingency plan for your business unit.

　Contingency planning is an outgrowth of the environmental analysis—the study of major issues that can affect your industry and your business. The preparation of alternative plans and contingency plans to be prepared for change and opportunity is a vital part of strategic planning. It helps us avoid surprises. It will be stressed more in future years in our strategic-planning process.

Exhibit 15: Instructions for Threats and Opportunities, Contingency Plans—A Machine and Tool Manufacturer

This section describes how our strategy would change under alternate versions of the future environment. The general purpose is to identify and discuss management's response in the event that the future environment of business conditions or of product or competitive position should be different from that which is assumed in our previously stated scenario.

Threats and Opportunities: Should only include those items which are strategic (those which can potentially change the order of things). But do not shortchange consideration of threats and opportunities. It is important for senior management to be aware of contingent events, their probability, how we could respond, and their impact.

Rating: Assess the significance of the threats and opportunities. Describe the potential impact in a few words (e.g., severe, moderate, etc.). Assign a probability and timing (e.g., low chance by 1983). Whether the issue is significant is a function of its potential impact, plus its probability and timing. Describe significance as low, very high, etc.

How We Will Remain Flexible: Which routes in the basic plan can we take that will not burn our bridges (should we have to respond to this alternate scenario)?

How General Policies and Plans Would Change: On an exception basis, describe how our policies and action programs would look.

Tracking Procedure: How will we monitor the situation? Do we have some early warning system to signal us?

What Triggers Our Alternate Response: What tangible, measurable set of events will convince us to act on our contingency plan?

---

been limited to a few contingencies which represent substantial deviations from planning assumptions."

Another participating company's planning guide directs its managers to give thought to what their contingency plans would be under certain conditions, such as: demand not meeting expectations, counterreaction of competition, unavailability of capital, significant rise in costs, and other possibilities.

Illustrations of how contingency planning is presented in planning manuals are shown in Exhibits 13, 14, and 15.

Focusing on Strategic Issues

If plans were developed without considering the key strategic issues facing the corporation or the business unit, they would be formulated in a vacuum. But although experienced managers are generally well aware of the critical concerns of their businesses, some may prove short-sighted about the larger environments and influences that affect their businesses. Many current planning procedures and documentation are, therefore, specifically designed to direct managers' attention to identifying and addressing the strategic issues affecting their units.

Incorporating a new focus on issues in the business-unit requirements of an aerospace manufacturer was a major significant change, according to its planning executive, because it changed the emphasis from "projected divisional financial performance to emphasizing division issues and strategies. We no longer require division financial projections and have reduced the strategic-planning document to a ten-page narrative." To encourage a more strategic focus in their planning efforts, a number of companies have built in a focus on issue identification in the planning process.

This factor may be addressed anywhere in the normal development of plans prior to the setting of strategies or strategic options. It is difficult to position the identification of issues in a formal sense. Although one food company advises its managers to begin their planning activity with the identification of key issues, other companies may insert this as a special section following the selection of objectives or the analysis of external trends and competitive situations. The aim is to ensure that managers identify key issues and attempt to respond to them during the course of developing a strategic plan. A pharmaceutical company, for example, explains: "Key issues should serve as the basis for developing strategic objectives. In other words, divisional objectives represent the strategic response to those issues that are expected to have a significant effect on future business."

Strategic issues are variously defined by different companies. They also vary according to organizational level. Here are some examples of how companies define this concept for their managers:

"A key issue may be defined as a single factor or set of factors which, if developed as expected, will have a significant impact (either positive or negative) on the future outcome of the planning entity. Key issues may have either an internal or an external orientation. The ability to recruit, hire and retain key managerial talent is an example of an internally oriented key issue. The ability of an industry area to find suitable means to grow in spite of an FTC order to cease acquisition activity provides an example of an externally oriented key issue."

—*A food company*

* * * * *

"A major issue is an issue important to the future profitability of the business unit which has not been resolved. These should be listed in order of priority for management attention. Major issues are not only those which might require corporate resources to resolve. Major issues are those topics on which business unit management should be initiating investigation in order to identify alternative directions and select a strategy."

—*An industrial equipment manufacturer*

* * * * *

"Business issues are those changes in the relationship among the company its customers, and competitors, or the industry environment, that will:

1. Change the existing market relationship (e.g., new customer needs, competitive costs, or key skills for the supplier).
2. Shift the competitive balance.
3. Define the major risks, opportunities and constraints you face.
4. Influence your chosen strategy.

"Business issues can be identified in several areas:

1. Technical shifts
2. Changing customer needs
3. Competitor activities
4. Business life cycle
5. Needed resources and skills

"What impact do these key issues have on our strategies, and how do we plan to address them in strategy formulation?"

—*An aircraft manufacturer*

* * * * *

The food company (in the first of the examples above) lists six key corporate issues which each group is asked to consider:

"1. *Base Business Vitality*—please direct special attention to what you intend to do to preserve the strength and vitality of your base businesses.

"2. *Real (Physical) Growth*—special emphasis will be given to physical volume growth. Please explain what you will be doing to stimulate physical volume increases in your businesses.

"3. *Capital Investment Requirements*—please include an assessment of your needs for new capital investment, focusing on the strategies for major new product or business areas.

"4. *Competitive Comparisons*—please analyze the strategic and financial performance of your major competitors and discuss how your strategies will assure successful performance in view of likely or possible competitive actions.

"5. *International Expansion*—as you did last year, please explore when, where and how potential international expansion might be attractive for your area.

"6. *Human Resource and Public Affairs*—please identify those human-resource and public-affairs trends which are likely to have the most significant impact on your businesses and describe your planned responses. All groups and business units should outline their management-development plans."

Business units are generally asked to develop their own sets of issues, and are frequently prompted by questions or examples to facilitate the process. A bank, for example, instructs its units to summarize the major strategic issues they face by framing them as questions for executive management's consideration, decision or for more detailed study.

In an unusual educational approach, a steel company sets forth a procedure for issue resolution. It introduces the subject by explaining two necessary elements: (1) the criteria which the solution must satisfy; and (2) the alternatives from which a solution will be decided. Minor issues, the plan format states, can be resolved using informal methods, basically dialogue. But other issues require a more rigorous treatment, it goes on, and recommends a formal procedure for dialogue. (See Exhibit 16.) The document points out that:

"Input from the general executives will be needed to establish decision criteria as well as to suggest various decision options. The output from the issue resolution phase should be a set of recommended decision options—options both relating to operating the existing business more profitably now or in the future, and to developing profitable business for the future. The goal-setting phase utilizes these options with appropriate documentation and dialogue to establish goals for each operating unit and the company as a whole."

Some Other Changes and Nonchanges

Many aspects of the planning process are undergoing discernible change, and there are indications that other areas are receiving closer scrutiny.

Planning for Staff and Support Units

While most companies largely limit the planning process to line or business-unit managers, several of the planning documents submitted for this study also include a request for plans by staff and support units, especially human-resource plans (see Exhibit 17). Such personnel plans detail, in the main, headcount requirements and skill needs over the next several years, and are not directly related to the development of strategic plans. Two companies, however, present two different strategic approaches to their human-resource planning. In one company, managers are requested to fill in a schedule with three columns: (1) identification of strategic plans having human-resource implications, (2) human-resource needs resulting from the plans, and (3) action planned to meet these needs. The types of strategic plans in the first column are to be identified from the following:

Exhibit 16: Instructions for Issue Resolution—A Steel Company

The following outline shows the basic steps in issue resolution. A brief and hypothetical example is used to illustrate the type of data required in each step.

STEP	EXAMPLE
(1) Issue definition (from previous phase)	(1) A projected decrease of market share of a product from 12% to 9% due to inability to manufacture product to new quality standards.
(2) Communication of issue to top management	(2) A concise statement of the issue (as in Step 1) together with background data. Name the specific individuals who have accountability for resolving the issue and an estimate of when this work will be completed.
(3) Establish criteria which the decision must attempt to satisfy	(3) Minimize new capital investment; no price reductions; solution must be able to achieve a market share of 10% minimum in two years; minimize loss of sales of other related products.
(4) Development of specific decision options.	(4) (a) Begin to phase out the market altogether. (b) Concentrate on particular segment of the market not requiring higher quality standards. (c) Accelerate development of new variants in the product line.
(5) Testing of decision options vis-a-vis selection criteria	(5) Options 4a and 4b satisfy two out of the four criteria but result in a significant loss in market share, and result in a high probability of loss of other business to major customers. Option 4c satisfies three out of the four criteria but would require a minimum of $30 million (with a projected aftertax return of 15%).
(6) Selection of best decision option	(6) Option 4c is chosen since it most closely satisfies the decision criteria and it represents an opportunity to expand company's market-share profitably through sales of a premium quality product.
(7) List major assumptions which underpin the decision option	(7) Increasing development funds by 50% will reduce development time to six months instead of two years; commercially produced product will perform at least as well as material produced to date; new-product costs will exceed standard product costs by no more than 3%; new investment will not exceed $30 million.
(8) Explain how decision would be implemented	(8) The expanded development budget would be used to increase the number of field tests plus attempting longer commercial runs (using existing equipment). After six months, results to date would be evaluated in order to determine if the project should be continued (and the capital investment made).
(9) Predict the probable financial results on total product line or total operations from implementing this decision	(9) Try to forecast at least growth in sales, net income, and total cash flow; also project capital requirements and net cash flow resulting directly from implementing the decision.
(10) Predict probable competitive responses	(10) Each of our competitors will undertake a concerted program to produce a similar product line. We anticipate that our lead time until competitive products appear to be at least 12 months. With this lead time and our excellent marketing channels, a market share of at least 15% is anticipated.
(11) Assess the total risk in achieving success	(11) Technical risk is the controlling factor and we estimate a 60% to 75% probability of success. Total risk in the project should be in the 50-60% range.

The data developed in this format will be directly applicable for use in the goal-setting phase.

Exhibit 17: Function Responsibilities and Plans Required—A Diversified Company

FUNCTION AREA	SUMMARY STATEMENT OF STRATEGIC DIRECTION	COMPLETE LONG-RANGE STRATEGIC PLAN, SUMMARY STATEMENT OF STRATEGIC DIRECTION
I Corporate Executive Office		
II Human Relations Development	X	X
Productivity Programs		
Human-Resource Planning and Development		X
Public Affairs		X
Compensation		
Organization Development		
Executive Development		X
Human-Resource Research		
III Personnel and Administration	X	X
Equal Opportunity Planning		
Staffing and Personnel Services		X
Labor Relations		
Personnel Planning		
IV Technology and Planning	X	X
Business Strategies		
Corporate Quality		
Applications and Product Strategy		X
Technology Programs		
Energy Programs		X
Technology Exchange		
Corporate Research		
V Finance	X	X
Tax		X
International Finance		X
Fiscal Planning		X
Operations Finance		X
Treasury		X
Internal Audit		
VI Corporate Services	X	
Legal		
Government Programs and International Trade		X
Government Affairs		X
Operation Services		
Real Estate and Facilities Administration		X
Business Ventures		
VII Corporate Marketing	X	X
Public Relations		X
Communication Services		X
Industry Marketing		X
Marketing Services		
Marketing Development		
Distributor Relations		
VIII Executive Office Staff		
IX Corporate Growth		
X Small Business Development		
XI Human Resource Management and Services		
XII Urban and Rural Ventures	—	—
Totals	6	24

"1. Expansion of existing businesses;
"2. Addition of new capacity (new plants, distribution facilities, etc.);
"3. Reduction or discontinuation of any current business activity;
"4. Ventures, acquisitions or divestitures;
"5. New product introduction;
"6. New technologies or applications;
"7. Changes in operating methods or procedures;
"8. Changes in organization structure."

The other company introduces human-resource issues to be considered and responded to. Among the issues it proposes are labor-force composition, employee-benefit and labor costs, employment security.

Planning Internationally

The impact of increased global competition takes a variety of forms in business, but it may not be apparent in planning processes at all. Many product divisions, for example, already have "global" business charters. Indeed "globalization" affects many divisions that already are worldwide, but affects them most in their domestic markets. Issues dealing with international competition or market standing, for instance, are incorporated in the unit's plan.

A broader international outlook is appearing in some of the companies in this study, but it is not stressed in their planning procedures, from the evidence submitted. In a section entitled, "International Marketplace," one manufacturing firm cautiously offers suggestions to its managers:

"It is believed that certain divisions have an opportunity to increase their sales base or reduce costs through expansion of markets or operations outside the United States. On the other hand, one of the corporate business principles states that international investments will not be made unless a market has been established through exporting products or technology or unless we have gained considerable knowledge of doing business through previous projects or programs. Therefore, possibilities for exporting products or technology or for participating in projects or programs should be reviewed and a brief narrative included in the plan for opportunities which should be investigated for expanding outside the United States and the possible benefits which could be achieved."

Only 48 of the 214 reporting companies recorded any change in the planning for international units during the past five years, but almost all of these said that they are now giving it greater emphasis. Most are manufacturing organizations, since a good many of the nonmanufacturing companies' operations are principally domestic units.

The major changes have had the purpose of integrating these international units into the company's total planning process. In many instances, these efforts are still in an evolutionary stage, starting, perhaps, with closer attention to economic projections abroad, particularly in countries with high inflation.

The area of international planning is receiving increased attention, according to survey participants, but many feel improvement is necessary.

Monitoring the Plan

Monitoring the progress of the implementation of the plan shows no really new developments in most of the companies. As reported elsewhere, most companies usually consider quarterly or monthly reviews of performance vis-à-vis plan as the measure of achievement, even though this may not accurately accord longer-term direction.[3]

Monitoring long-term direction of the firm remains a troublesome and frustrating exercise. Several companies use milestones to mark progress, while others have expanded the monitoring of objectives and their achievement, or have initiated stronger follow-up procedures. (See Exhibits 45, 46 and 47.)

A few companies report continued difficulties in linking their operating plans to the budget, and are attempting procedures that will more closely mesh these two stages of the firm's planning process.

[3]Rochelle O'Connor, *Tracking The Strategic Plan*. The Conference Board, Report No. 830. 1983.

Chapter 3

Planning Documentation and Formats

THE MOST NOTICEABLE changes in the planning process are in the prescribed formats for documenting the strategic plans. According to more than 70% of the reporting companies, these changes show a definite trend toward more flexibility, greater simplification, and a shift in focus to issues and strategies from a former financial emphasis.

Also, as the corporate planning unit in many companies has been relieved of some responsibilities, there has been a significant concern over planning in the business units. To attend to these new needs, a number of companies state that planning requirements have been adapted to individual business units to a far greater extent than former standardization permitted.

"We tailored the requirements to the particular needs of each division so that reviews are geared to issues and decisions," says the planning executive of a large food processing firm. An oil company wants a breakdown by business segment "independent of organizational or accounting centers," and issues its instructions accordingly.

There has been a decided move among many of the companies toward a loosened, less structured system of documentation that lessens specific requirements and encourages an approach that is more reflective of business issues. Several planning guides stress that, aside from some necessary requirements, business units may choose the format most suitable for their needs and situation to document their planning. An industrial products company, for example, announces:

"Note that for the written plan, considerable freedom in format is encouraged so that we continually evolve toward better ways of communicating the essentials of the business plan. The text may be a terse listing of points or it may be written paragraphs of prose. Charts and tables may be used to supply additional information. Special topics may be dwelt on in depth in some years and referred to in subsequent plans."

And a business forms manufacturer's manual states:

"The written document should be brief, clear and persuasive. Recognizing that each division has a *different* story to tell in its *own* way, as the product of a *unique* team effort, this guide purposely does *not* intend to be prescriptive on how brevity, clarity and persuasiveness are achieved."

One company is now experimenting with a format that allows free-form answers to six questions (see box). Together with the new flexibility, there is a move toward simplification and a reduction in the amount of detail required. Some companies say that they have cut back former "voluminous" submissions by focusing their guidelines to minimize excess information. Restricting input, according to some of the respondents, has resulted in more meaningful analysis and concise statements that form a better basis for management decisions. (See Exhibit 18.)

"This year's instruction packet is much thinner than in the recent past," a chemical firm announces. "Thus, it reflects a reduction in what is required to be submitted and is intended to reinforce the desire that the long-range plan documents be kept brief and meaty." One company's terse remark: "We simplified everything."

But simplifying planning requirements and reducing the amount of material submitted serves a larger purpose than producing more easily portable plan books. Like the short letter that takes so much more time to write, the new conciseness that is sought is based largely on a redirection of emphasis toward a more qualitative and less financial focus.

Although several companies comment that they are maintaining a strong focus on the financial data in their planning formats, most of the others that reported on their changes in this area say they are much more concerned now with issues, strategies and implementation. An insurance company executive points out that his firm's planning process had been "formalistic, extrapolative. Now the format is meaningless; it is substance that counts."

The financial requirements in a mining machinery

Divisional Strategic Planning Questions to be Addressed—
A Metal Products Company

1. How will your division play its part in implementing the corporate mission statement?

The recently published mission statement was developed to provide strategic direction for the corporation. For the corporation to achieve its mission, a cooperative and participative effort is required, both of the corporate office as it manages its portfolio of business and of the divisions as they carry out their related missions.

2. What should the corporation be able to expect from your division?

Many corporations are very specific as to exactly what is expected of each division and the basis upon which divisional performance is to be measured. Some of these expectations and measurements can be stated in financial terms such as profitabilty, return on assets, cash flow, etc. Others are nonfinancial and may relate to the world economy, the business cycle, providing a nursery for talent, etc. Care must be taken that the expectations are not mutually exclusive.

As you answer the question, please indicate what might be expected of your division, in light of history; what you believe corporate should be able to expect and the specific actions that you will take to effectuate your intentions.

3. In what ways will your operations respond to change in the business environment?

Some business leaders have predicted that U.S. business will emerge from the recession fundamentally different from the way that it entered the recession. Some of the reasons given include increased off-shore sourcing of components, heightened foreign penetration in many areas of finished goods, world energy prices, consumers' hesitancy to increase spending, and many others. Without limiting your discussion to any of the above areas, please comment on the above question.

4. What competitive advantages will you enjoy and how will you capitalize on them?

Much effort has been focused in the past strategic-planning activities on identifying competitors and analyzing their competitive strengths and weaknesses. The information derived in this evaluation provided insight into the relative ability of each competitor to compete in the marketplace. The main shortcoming in this kind of evaluation is that it fails to draw conclusions concerning specific strategic moves that need to be undertaken.

As you address this question, another point to consider is your competitive weaknesses and how they will be minimized.

5. What are the expectations of your customers and the end users and how will you meet their needs?

As a company fine-tunes its offerings of products and services, one of the most important pieces of information to be considered is the needs of customers and end users. To be successful, there must be a match between the requirements of the marketplace and the products and services being offered. For example, a company may offer "off-the-shelf" kinds of products while the market is looking for highly sophisticated engineering capabilities. Obviously, the reverse of this example is also valid. To achieve the necessary matching of these factors, a thorough understanding must be developed as to the <u>real</u> needs of the marketplace.

6. What will be the most significant strategic issues to be faced by your division and how will you respond to them?

Because of the diverse nature of the company's divisions, the response to this question will vary, division by division. Please reflect upon the various critical issues that you expect your division to face over the next five years and then select from one to three issues that will have the greatest impact. For each issue, consider appropriate strategic ways to respond to it.

---

manufacturing company have been reduced significantly. This has been done for a variety of reasons, its planning guide states, including: "To reduce the workload on the field accounting function; to recognize emphasis on strategic and operational actions rather than accounting details; in recognition of spotty credibility of some past projections." And a major food processor says the company has experienced major change by "deleting 'budget' and initiating an issues-driven format."

The redesign of planning formats usually reflects the kinds of changes in strategic thinking that the firm desires. Thus, simplification of planning may also take the form, as it does in a West Coast bank, for example, of "less verbiage, more quantification." Planning guidelines and documentation are the vehicles that lend themselves well to this effort.

This is how two contributing planners characterize the new planning focus in their companies:

Exhibit 18: A New Emphasis in the Planning Process—A Diversified Machinery Manufacturer

The New Planning Process
The company's planning process has changed in two fundamental ways:

- First, the planning process now emphasizes thought:

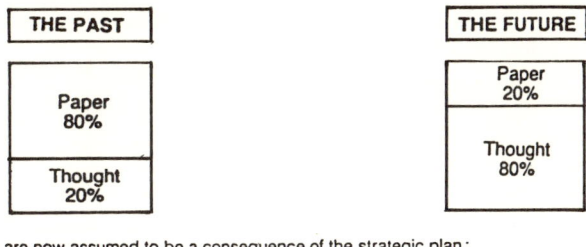

- Second, financial results are now assumed to be a consequence of the strategic plan.

The goal of planning is to create the future, not to forecast it.

"The plan narrative content has been significantly curtailed. In most cases, standard forms have been substituted. These changes have been incorporated because we realized individuals responsible for the plan were concentrating on 'style and management interpretation' of the plan narrative rather than on the issues or business environment confronting their business segments.

"The forms are structured to force unit-division management to think through various basic business parameters prior to preparing their plans, and, secondly, to provide an outline for the plan format. Although not required, it is encouraged that the forms be included in the final plan submission and be utilized in presenting the background and rationale for the plan during the management review sessions. This area is considered the most important change made in the past four years."
—*An industrial products manufacturer*

* * *

"Probably the greatest change has been greater emphasis on informal communication and follow-up throughout the year to make sure that key strategic issues are raised and addressed and that the highest priority items receive the required attention. There is greater emphasis on keeping the number of strategies and issues to a minimum, concentrating on those that are most important. There is greater emphasis on strategic thinking by corporate and divisional management."
—*An automotive equipment company*

* * *

Other companies have, of course, instituted other kinds of changes and refinements that they believe will improve the quality of plans; and several companies change their formats every year, either to focus emphasis on current issues and needs, or routinely, as a publisher reports, "to counter boredom." A high-technology planner remarks that the prescribed formats "are always changed and always remain the same in essence."

* * *

Recent planning documents and formats show an increased use of educational materials to instruct and explain planning procedures and techniques to business unit managers. Glossaries of planning terms abound and where a glossary is not supplied, instructions tend to be quite explicit.

Worksheets are used by a number of companies to help business-unit managers analyze data and develop plans. In most cases, these worksheets are used to develop strategy, but are not required to be submitted with the plan.

Other helpful aids furnished to managers are tutorials, reading suggestions and references, samples of hypothetical plans, and explanations of analysis techniques and types of strategies. Some use highly sophisticated planning techniques, explained in a professional manner. Other companies, mindful perhaps of their managers' distrust of a "planning mystique," have kept their instructions more simple and phrased in the language of general business management.

The balance of this chapter is devoted to exhibits illustrating the sequential development of a typical business-unit strategic plan. They were selected to show examples of the many ways in which the planning guides lead managers through the planning process. The principal changes over the past few years, discussed in Chapter 2, are evident in many of the exhibits. They may be compared with those which appear in a previous report, "Corporate Guides to Long-Range Planning," in which the various elements of the plan are discussed fully.[1] Financial schedules have been excluded deliberately.

[1]O'Connor, 1976.

Exhibit 19: Practical Exercises for the Manager—A Diversified Machinery Manufacturer

An Introduction to Practical Exercises 7, 8 and 9—

It is 9:15 on a Sunday morning. As happens every Sunday morning, you wake up, swing your feet over the side of the bed and plant them firmly on the floor. There you sit for a few minutes, head in hand, staring out the window.

It's raining and chilly outside. The weather gives you a perfect excuse to spend your Sunday doing exactly what you like to do best—curl up in front of the fire to read the Sunday paper.

You get out of bed, put on your bathrobe, and head for the kitchen. You pour a cup of coffee. You lay the fire and light it. All you need now is the two Sunday papers to which you regularly subscribe—off to the front door. You open the door and....

PRACTICAL EXERCISE #7

The first newspaper you pick up has three headlines in bold black print. The story behind each threatens the ability of your business to *supply products*. The articles could deal with any of a number of subjects—the availability of raw materials, components, labor or professional managers...each of which is vitally important to the future success of your business. What are the three worst headlines that you might read which would affect the ability of your business to *supply* products?

1. _____

2. _____

3. _____

PRACTICAL EXERCISE #8

After reading the headline of the first paper, you stagger, trying to collect your thoughts, hoping that the second newspaper will have a happier headline. This is not to be, however—no peace for the wicked, no rest for the weary. You look down at the second paper and, like the first one, it contains three headlines which foretell disaster for your business. This time, however, each headline spells disaster for the *demand for your products*. What are the three worst headlines that you could read?

1. _____

2. _____

3. _____

PRACTICAL EXERCISE #9

You stagger back into the house and close the door behind you. Your hopes of spending a restful, lazy day in front of the fire are now shattered. But, like Ebenezer Scrooge on Christmas morning, an idea comes to you in a flash—"Maybe I can do something." You race back to the bedroom, get dressed, and dash off to the office to start to work on avoiding these disasters. When you get to the office you write down those actions you will begin on Monday morning to avert these disasters. What three actions do you write down to avert each set of disasters?

ACTIONS TO ASSURE CONTINUED SUPPLY OF PRODUCTS (See Practical Exercise #7)

1. _____

2. _____

3. _____

ACTIONS TO ASSURE CONTINUED DEMAND FOR PRODUCTS (See Practical Exercise #8)

1. _____

2. _____

3. _____

Additional Exhibits

	Page
Contents of Planning Manuals	30
Plan Outlines and Contents	32
Executive Summary	33
Mission Statement	35
External Analysis	36
Internal Analysis	39
Goals and Objectivs	41
Strategies	44
Action Programs	48

Contents of Planning Manuals

Exhibit 20: Contents of Planning Manual—A Packaging Manufacturer

(Note: Sections I through VI should be prepared for each Strategic Business Unit)

	Page

I. Analysis of the Competitive Environment
   A. Introduction
   B. Review of Competitive Forces
	1

II. Analysis of Competitive Strength	3

III. Charter
   A. Basis for Competing
   B. Business Definition
   C. Competitive Advantage
   D. Relative Return on Invested Capital
   E. Competitive Position
	4

IV. Business Principles	9

V. Strategy and Plan
   A. Strategic Intention
   B. Strategic Issues
   C. Business Plan
	10

VI. SBU Financial Implications
   A. Financial Targets
   B. SBU Financial Projection
   C. Major Assumptions
	12

VII. Division or Group Summary
   A. Financial Targets and Objectives
   B. Division or Group Business Plan
	14

VIII. Financial Implications	15
IX. Building Blocks	23

X. Other
   A. Innovation
   B. International Marketplace
	24

Appendix A - Checklist of Competitive Forces

Appendix B - Basis for Competing

Appendix C - Strategy Checklist

Glossary

Exhibit 21: Long-Range Strategic Plan—A Computer Hardware and Services Company

MAJOR SECTION	CONTENTS	PURPOSE
SUMMARY STATEMENT OF STRATEGIC DIRECTION	o Summary Statement of Strategic Direction	An Executive Summary
OUR NATURE TODAY	o Charter Definition...Today	What we are today

	o External Environment
	   Comparative Peer Companies
	   Technology
	   Assumption of Change	

	o Internal Environment
	   Current Services and Processes
	   Technology
	   Services in Development
	   Physical Resources
	   Human Resources
	   Innovation
	   Key Success Factors
	   Strengths and Needs	

	o Charter Definition...1987	What we will become

(continued)

Exhibit 21: Long-Range Strategic Plan — A Computer Hardware and Services Company (continued)

FUNCTION OBJECTIVES	o Corporate Driven, Line Organization Driven, Other Forces Driven Objectives	What we plan to make happen
	o Summary—Direction Changes from Previous Plan	
	o Summary—Planned Financial and Headcount Performance Results –Function Direct Managed –Line Organization Managed	
HALFTIME	Review and Adjust to Concurrence	Verbally achieve agreement on direction
STRATEGIES	o Action strategies o Key Risks and Exposures o Strategy Changes from Previous Plan	How we plan to do it
IMPLEMENTATION REQUIREMENTS	o Organization Impacts o Human resource Impacts o Capital Equipment & Facilities o Information Systems Needs o Dependencies on other organizations o Other	What it will take
CONTROLLING TO PLAN	o Monitoring External Environment o Measuring Progress Against Objectives o Plan Adjustment	How we will control
RESPONSE TO ISSUES	o Line Organization Issues o Top Strategic Issues	How we will manage their effect on us
QUESTIONS FOR OPERATIONS		What I need to know
LRSP SUPPLEMENTAL REQUIREMENTS	o As Required	

Plan Outlines and Contents

Exhibit 22: Components of Planning System—A Medical Products Firm

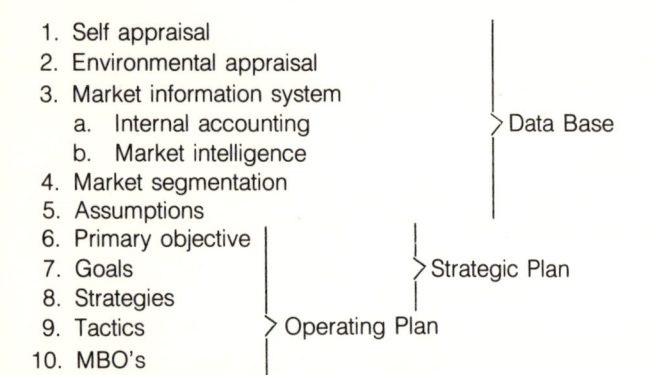

1. Self appraisal
2. Environmental appraisal
3. Market information system
   a. Internal accounting   ⎫
   b. Market intelligence   ⎬ Data Base
4. Market segmentation   ⎪
5. Assumptions   ⎪
6. Primary objective   ⎪
7. Goals   ⎬ Strategic Plan
8. Strategies   ⎪
9. Tactics   ⎫ Operating Plan
10. MBO's   ⎭
11. Impact of facilities   Capital Appropriations Budget
12. Impact on Personnel
13. Impact on Information Systems (Data Processing)

Exhibit 23: Plan Outline—An Industrial Products Manufacturer

I. Situation Analysis
   - The Market
   - The Product
   - The Competition

II. Environmental Assumptions
   - The Economy
   - Technology
   - The Competition

III. Overall Strategic Thrust
   - Competitive Goals
   - Financial Goals
   - Investment Requirements

IV. Risk Assessment
   - Alternative Scenarios
   - Contingency Thresholds and Plans
   - Linkages or Synergies

V. Analysis
   - Past Performances vs. Past Strategy
   - Testing Assumptions
   - Cash Results

A Manager's Strategy Narrative will describe the vital issues in each of these areas and how the business unit will confront them so that resources invested will generate the required return commensurate with the risk.

Exhibit 24: Plan Contents—A Transportation Company

- Executive Summary
- Discussion of Business and Financial Goals
- Situation Analysis and Forecasts
  - Economic
  - Markets
  - Financial
  - Competition (Narrative and Forecast)
  - Political
  - Human Resources
  - Internal Strengths and Weaknesses
- Competitive Profiles (Individual Carriers)
- Deployments
- Key Issues, Objectives and Strategies
- Risks and Contingencies
- Business Development Opportunities

Exhibit 25: Plan Outline—A High-Technology Products Manufacturer

I. Management Summary

II. Business Definition
   - Mission
   - Purpose
   - Role

III. Progress Report
   - Comparison of key financial and market indicators
   - Progress made on major strategies

IV. Market and Customer Analysis
   - Potential versus served market
   - Market segmentation

V. Competitive Analysis
   - Description of three major competitors
   - Analysis of competitors' strategies

VI. Objectives, Strategies and Programs
   - Key objectives
   - Major strategies to accomplish the objectives
   - Action programs to implement strategies
   - Major assumptions and contingency programs
   - Market share matrix

VII. Financial Projections
   - Financial projections statement
   - Personnel projections

Executive Summary

Exhibit 26: One-Page Plan Summary—An Industrial Products Manufacturer

DEFINITION

Define the business area in terms of products and markets. Explicitly identify the major customer groups and the primary customer functions served (i.e., what needs does the product satisfy?). Also state the "key success factors" which are necessary.

PROFITABILITY

How profitable is the business? Is the level of profitability considered acceptable? What factors are affecting the trends in profitability? What is the profitability outlook? What has to happen before acceptable profitability can be achieved?

MARKET AND INDUSTRY

How large is the market? What is its growth rate? What trends are influencing demand? What is the stage of life cycle (rapid growth, mature, declining)? In the United States as well as foreign markets? Provide explicit statements on export, licensing and foreign investment opportunities, either positive or negative.

COMPETITIVE POSITION

What is the competitive environment? Who is the competition? What are the competitive market shares? What are the relative strengths and weaknesses? How is the competitive environment changing? What factors are likely to alter our competitive position? Where applicable, we would like explicit comments on the changing nature of foreign competition.

STRATEGIC THRUST

This should be a one- or two-sentence summary of the strategic objective statement which should express the overall approach to the management of the business.

Exhibit 27: Executive Comment—An Information Services Corporation

The purpose of this section is to state your strategy briefly, and to comment on any points that you consider to be of particular importance to your business. Since this section is your opportunity to highlight the key points of the plan as a whole, we suggest that you prepare it *after* completing all other sections.

State your strategy for each principal business in terms of the competitive position you are aiming for by the end of the plan period. Whether this goal involves a change or simply maintaining your present position, indicate how you will deploy your resources to achieve the desired result. You may wish to stress one or two points of particular strategic concern to you (e.g., the adequacy of certain resources, or the competitive risks associated with implementing the proposed strategy).

Please note that we are seeking your comments and insights concerning the plan as a whole, rather than a reiteration of the remaining sections.

Exhibit 28: Executive Summary—A Construction Company

A. *Group Executive's Letter* summarizes the group's strategic plan. The letter should be addressed to the chief executive officer and be signed by the group executive. All items should be precise or quantified. Do not duplicate commentary or data presented in the exhibits or profit centers' plans. The letter should include those items the writer feels are most appropriate but, as a minimum, should include:

(1) Charter, principal objectives, supporting strategies and action steps for the group, including those that are applicable to more than one business center.

(2) Discussion of the critical issues that are expected to affect the group's strategy and profitability in its markets.

(3) Description and rationale for developing possible proposed businesses or technologies not covered by profit center plans.

(4) Broad support for proposed capital expenditure priorities.

Please be brief—not more than five pages, preferably fewer.

B. Exhibits

The following exhibits should be referred to as appropriate in support of the group executive's letter.

(1) Financial and personnel summary.

(2) Ranking of expansion and development projects for the group and profit centers.

(3) Profiles of major expansion and development proposals (other than those identified in the profit center plans).

Items 2 and 3 should include technology-oriented programs. Provide the best estimate concerning resource requirements for these programs (capital, people, etc.).

Use the exhibit forms and instructions provided.

Exhibit 29: Executive Summary—An Industrial Products Firm

When the long-range plan is completed and ready for submittal to corporate management, this section is prepared and inserted at the beginning of the written long-range plan.

The summary serves as an initial presentation of the plan, after which corporate executives can examine more closely those portions that they wish to probe in detail.

This section should provide a brief historical biography of the business area where pertinent, and a brief statement regarding the future direction and objective recommended for the business area (such as expansion, continuing at present level, planned phase-out or divestment, etc.). The section should contain a brief statement regarding the key elements of strategy (such as new product development, application of additional capital and other resources, increased production and facilities, etc.). It should contain a brief statement of key issues and risks that can influence the successful achievement of the strategy. It should contain a brief statement relative to priorities and to the expected payoff if the strategy (or strategies) is undertaken. And it should contain a brief statement to help validate the essential reasons why this direction and strategy is the correct one to follow.

Mission Statement

Exhibit 30: Mission Statement—An Insurance Company

Standard Process

This statement first explains the business you are in, or want to be in. It stakes out the arena in which your business unit is chartered to operate. Second, the mission identifies the unit's stakeholders. Stakeholders are groups of people who stand to gain or lose from your actions. For example, your shareholders, employees, customers, regulators and the general public. Finally, the mission spells out the business unit's responsibilities to its stakeholders.

The stakeholder concept is vitally important to the strategic planning process. We are not planning for ourselves—or even for an abstraction like a corporation. We are planning for people — people who have an investment in what we do. Put yourself in their shoes throughout your planning activity. Consider your objectives and decisions with them in mind.

The mission statement is the starting point for strategic planning. The goals that you develop should be compatible with your mission.

The mission statement should be concise and meaningful; no more than one page.

1983 Activity

Each unit is asked to review only briefly the mission they have established in former years. Unless your unit is entering into new business areas, there is little need for new work on your mission statement.

Exhibit 31: Mission Statement—A Telecommunications Company

The purpose of the mission statement is to express the underlying design, aim, purpose and thrust of a business entity based on the situation analysis and discussion with upper management. Each business unit, group, functional department and the company as a whole has a mission, so each should have a written mission statement. This statement should be available for review in the conference documents, but should not be covered in detail in the conference unless changes have been or should be made. This statement, as well as the rest of the business plan, should be viewed as a contract with executive management that should not be changed without their approval.

The mission statement is the first and most general component of a business plan. It should describe the parameters of the business, providing general direction on the role of the business and its scope of operations.

The mission statement has two parts:

- **Guiding concept**—a single, short statement of the inspirational goal of the business. It should be something that all employees can grasp as the essence of their culture, yet describe the value being provided to the customer. Examples include AT&T's focus on telephone service quality and IBM's focus on computing innovation.

- **Mission**—about a half-page that tells *what* you want to be. The points that should be covered vary with the level in the hierarchy of the company since the role and scope are different for each level. The following are brief topic outlines for each of the three major levels.

Mission Statement Profiles

Corporate	Group	Business unit
Guiding Concept	**Guiding Concept**	**Guiding Concept**
Mission	**Mission**	**Mission**
Scope of operations – Maximizing shareholder value – Value provided to customer – Industries/major markets – Geographic areas Corporate center role (value provided to corporation) – Portfolio management – Resource allocation – Synergy management – Corporate development – Executive management development Social policies	Scope of operations – Markets – Position targeted in markets – Geographic areas Group role (value provided to corporation and BU's) – Fulfillment of role in corporate portfolio – Portfolio management – Synergy management – Resource allocation – Group development	Scope of operations – Markets/segments served – Customer needs filled – Products provided – Functions performed (manufacture, distribute, service, etc.) – Position targeted in markets – Geographic areas Business unit role (value provided to group and corporation) – Fulfillment of role in group portfolio – Market development – Business/product development – Distribution development – Resource management – Operations management

ADDITIONAL EXHIBITS

External Analysis

Exhibit 32: External Situation Analysis—An Industrial Products Manufacturer

The external business environment plays a significant role in our day-to-day affairs. Some of these external factors present opportunities and others adversely impact our operations.

Please comment on those external factors which have or threaten to have a substantial positive or negative effect on your business. Emphasize the impact of these external factors on the areas of your business through which strategies are implemented and objectives are achieved. This should be no more than three pages, any additional data can be included in an appendix.

A checklist of major environmental categories appears below. Each category has some examples of items which could have an effect on one or more of our operations.

Technical

    Electronic controls, electric car, water hydraulics, solar energy, standardization.

Political

    Tax laws, OSHA, EEO, consumerism, pending legislation.

Economic

    Business cycle, money supply, inflation, consumer confidence, new fiscal and monetary policies, availability and cost of basic inputs including labor.

Physical

    Pollution, safety, health, disaster—potential flood, earthquake.

Social

    Local or national attitudes, involvement with community, degree of financial support of social organizations.

Energy Crisis

    Costs and availability: coal? oil? fuel oil? electricity?

Others—Specify and Discuss

Exhibit 33: External Trends and Analysis—A Toiletries and Cosmetics Firm

Critical Environmental Trends

Consistent with prior-year plan discussions, the business unit should identify where the most significant changes in the relevant operating environment are likely to take place over the next five years. Consider as appropriate:
— Technology (in terms of affecting product design as well as product utilization)
— Government regulatory trends
— Demographics
— National economic trends
— Life-style
— Distribution patterns
— Foreign competition

Competitor Analysis Summary

In addition to last year's competitive requirements, this year's summary includes an analysis of relative competitor characteristics. This form captures the quantifiable aspects of strategy and relates them to the SBU's top three competitors to communicate a clearer understanding of current and future strategic direction.

As with all the summary analyses included in the SBU plans, the forms in no way represent a comprehensive analysis. The competitive analysis intended to be developed here is the one with the most insights into understanding the competitors' probable future strategies, not the most facts.

Exhibit 34: Market Analysis Instructions—A Bank Holding Company

DETERMINING THE PLACEMENT OF A MARKET SEGMENT ON THE SEGMENT PORTFOLIO MATRIX

This form centers around a nine-cell market segment portfolio matrix which visually defines the business unit's current and planned future position in a market segment. The matrix has two dimensions: *future attractiveness* of a market segment (high, medium, low), and *your current and planned future market position* in that segment (strong, average, weak):

EXAMPLE

( ) = current market position
← = investment strategy
0 = planned future

To determine those served market segments where a particular level of investment of resources will pay off best (long term or short term), to close the gap between current and planned future market positions in each segment, you need to assess:

- The future attractiveness of the market segment. (Where do I want to be?)
- Your current competitive position. (Where am I now?)

1. Your assessment of the *future attractiveness of the market segment* requires you to evaluate a number of factors:
   a. Growth of market segment (life cycle)
   b. Profitability of current suppliers to segment
   c. Customer structure (total segment)
   d. Competitive structure
   e. Economic and financial structure
   f. Others you consider significant

Note: A market segment should be considered attractive if its potential (future) for providing a significant contribution to corporate objectives for earnings growth and ROI is judged to be high.

2. Your assessment of your *current competitive position* in a served market segment depends on your evaluation of:
   a. Trend in our volume of business and customers
   b. Market share and relative share
   c. Profitability
   d. Customer structure
   e. Products and services
   f. Rate of innovation
   g. Relative differentiation from competition
   h. Others you consider significant

Note. Competitive position in a served market segment is *strong* if you have a profitable, large share of the served market segment and specific characteristics which give you significant advantages over competitors in maintaining or improving this position.

DETERMINING MARKET SEGMENT INVESTMENT STRATEGIES

Strategy	Typical Matrix Placement and Characteristics of Market Segment	General Objective	Investment Commitment	Pay Out	Near Term Impact Vol.	ROI
I. Grow or Penetrate	Significant long-term earnings opportunity in high-growth segment.	Penetrate market to establish strong future position.	Sustained long-term investment. Accept high investment risk.	Long (5-7 yrs.)	↑	↓
II. Grow or Balanced	Significant current *and* long-term earnings and growth in mature market.	Maintain current strong position in market with little or no reduction in ROI.	Sustain investment at same rate as market. Accept medium investment risk.	Short to Medium (3-5 yrs.)	↑	→
III. Selective Investment	Significant current and future earnings in stable, low-growth market.	Maintain or improve ROI. Exploit selective opportunities for volume growth if available. Seek cost efficiencies.	Limited investments in targets of opportunity. Accept low investment risk.	Short (1-3 yrs.)	→	→
IV. Defend	Significant current earnings. Declining margin. Limited volume growth.	Defend earnings base until attractive alternative opportunities are developed.	Investment only in response to competitive inroads. Accept medium investment risk.	Short	→	↓

ADDITIONAL EXHIBITS

Exhibit 34: Market Analysis Instructions—A Bank Holding Company (continued)

V. Harvest	Significant current earnings from strong position in a flat or declining market; attractive alternatives available.	Maximize current earnings. Allow gradual erosion in share if it improves margin.	Disinvest gradually at a rate to avoid collapse of business.		↓ ↑
VI. Restructure or Rebuild	Deteriorated current earnings, despite strong share in significant market, due to internal shortcomings.	Correct internal deficiencies to restore profitability	One-time investment dictated by nature of deficiencies. Accept medium investment risk.	Short	→ ↓
VII. Withdraw	Declining market and earnings. Possible one-time earnings increment from sale or elimination of loss.	Withdraw from market on most favorable terms.	Disinvest	---	--- ---
VIII. Hold	Nature of opportunity not established	Develop strategy while maintaining status quo.	No investment until strategy developed.	---	--- ---

Exhibit 35: Situation Analysis—An Industrial Products Manufacturer

EXTERNAL ANALYSIS

A. Market

1. Customer identification (type and size)
2. Customer attitudes and buying habits
3. Key factors in selling market
    a. Design
    b. Appearance
    c. Price
    d. Distribution
    e. Service
    f. Volume production, etc.
4. Geographic location (if appropriate) and trends
5. Size—total sales potential
6. Growth trends and forecasts
7. Technological changes and trends
8. Changes in demand, requirements, distribution, etc.
9. International opportunities
10. New need identification (an unsatisfied need that could be satisfied with a new or existing product).

B. Competition

(Analyze the top four suppliers in your market segment—include yourself in top four.)

1. Who and where located?
2. Privately or publicly owned?
3. How long in business in this product line?
4. Major product lines
5. Size—total sales and sales in competing product line
6. Market share of sales
7. Business philosophy (price, quality, service, aggressive, docile, etc.)
8. Promotional efforts
9. Method of selling (direct, reps, agents, distributors, etc.)
10. Technological position or uniqueness
11. Methods of distribution (stocking distributors, branches, warehouses, etc.)

Exhibit 35: Situation Analysis—An Industrial Products Manufacturer (continued)

12. Financial data
    a. Net profit/sales ratio
    b. Return on investment
    c. Number of employees
    d. Facilities—size, own, rent, etc.
13. Their future outlook
14. Strengths and weaknesses
15. Current strategies
16. Cost and pricing factors
17. Threats to the future of your product line.

In compiling data on competitors, a serious and concentrated effort must be made. Where specific data are not available, use your best estimate and so note. If you cannot make an estimate, then indicate "don't know." Needless to say, there will be varying numbers of "don't knows" from competitor to competitor. These will point out the areas for future efforts at developing data.

C. Political, Economic and International Policies. (Those which have had an impact in the past or could have in the future on the product line.)

1. Economic trends, developments and forecasts
2. Government regulations
3. Political and social developments
4. National and international policies.

Internal Analysis

Exhibit 36: Situation Analysis—A Pharmaceuticals Company

The purpose of the situation analysis is to provide an in-depth review of each business as it exists today. Primary emphasis should be placed on an appraisal of each business unit's strengths and weaknesses, <u>as compared to competition</u>, and the problems and opportunities you will confront over the next several years in order to develop or maintain meaningful competitive differentiation.

The process involved in preparing a realistic situation analysis must include careful consideration of both qualitative and quantitative aspects of the competitive marketplace.

In a qualitative sense, you must first identify who you compete with, and then consider how your present business fares against this competition. In other words, "how are we better than our major business adversaries and in what ways are we weaker?" Some reference points to be considered include:

- Product lines—breadth and depth
- Marketing programs and advertising strength
- Target audience penetration
- Retailer-wholesaler relationships, distribution policies
- Field force size and ability
- New product development and process improvement
- Personnel and organization
- Administrative costs and productivity
- Adequacy of facilities, production capacity
- Pricing
- Other

<u>Quantitatively</u>, the competitive environment is best described by identifying overall market share, and further explaining this by identifying the market shares of the major products and lines. Although often difficult to isolate, the development of market-share data is essential for determining your current status and future growth and profitability potential.

If routine sources of market data (e.g., IMS, Nielsen) cannot be easily obtained, then one of the following methods should be used to describe market position:

- Relative market shares (i.e., your product and business sales as a percent of the sales of only the three largest competitors in that market).
- A comparison of your sales to the total company sales of all competitors in each market.
- A verbal description of the market franchise held by each major product or line (e.g., "dominant," "strong," "good," "fair" or "weak"). Since these or comparable phrases also provide additional insight to conventional market-share figures, include such descriptions in the discussion of market position.

(continued)

Exhibit 36: Situation Analysis—A Pharmaceuticals Company (continued)

It is important, also, to evaluate the markets in which your products compete. Each industry or business segment should be examined as to its attractiveness, both at present and in the future. A major consideration is market growth—are the products involved in high-growth markets, moderate, low or declining markets. Other considerations are: market profitability, vulnerability to inflation, cyclicality, pricing flexibility, and technology dependence.

Format

The situation analysis should be presented in narrative form, with market-share data included in the text or appended accordingly.

Exhibit 37: Internal Analysis—An Industrial Products Manufacturer

Please comment on the internal strengths, weaknesses, opportunities and threats (defined below) which your business faces today and is likely to encounter over the planning horizon. In doing so imagine that you are buying the division. What are the unique resources of the organization that can be capitalized on to improve profitability and/or rate of growth? What are the cracks in the organization that hamper your ability to take advantage of opportunities or adequately meet competition? By standing back and objectively viewing the present state of the division you will be able to isolate those factors which must be given consideration in future plans.

Much more detail may be developed in this analysis than should be included in the written plan. Identify those strengths, weaknesses, opportunities and threats with the most profit potential or leverage and concentrate on them. Include only those items which help explain strategic and tactical decisions. The statements should be terse and brief. They should identify the major, fundamental factors but not all of their symptoms and previous causes. The analysis can be four pages; supporting data can be included in an appendix.

- Strengths - Those things we are good at and should make the most of.
- Weaknesses - Things we do poorly and should correct or avoid. These are the internal factors that may keep us from reaching our objectives.
- Opportunities - Circumstances or conditions we could or should be taking advantage of but currently are not.
- Threats - Those negative situations that might come about if corrective or preventive measures are not taken.

A checklist of areas upon which you should comment appears below.

1. Market and Competition

    a. Pricing
    b. Delivery
    c. Warehousing
    d. Distribution
    e. Customers
    f. New products and markets
    g. Advertising and promotion
    h. Purchasing

2. Manufacturing

    a. New plant and equipment
    b. Productivity
    c. Quality control
    d. Cost reduction
    e. Raw materials
    f. Capacity utilization
    g. Personnel

3. Research and Development

    a. Process improvement
    b. Product development

4. Financial

    a. Inventory turnover—How has inventory turnover improved in the last two years? How could a 25% increase be achieved over the planning cycle?
    b. Accounts receivable—days outstanding: How and why have the days outstanding improved or worsened over the last two years?
    c. What specific actions will you take compared with your current approach, to make a significant improvement in collection of accounts receivable?

5. General

    a. Organization changes
    b. Labor relations
    c. Training
    d. Business systems development
    e. Communications
    f. Environmental and safety
    g. Planning—short term
    h. Budgeting
    i. International operations
    j. Public relations
    k. Other areas not specified above

Exhibit 38: Internal Analysis—A Medical Products Firm

Self-Appraisal

The management of each business center, division, company and business should have a good understanding of its strengths and weaknesses. Of particular importance is identifying those strengths and weaknesses that produce advantages or disadvantages vis-à-vis the competition. Listed below are some examples of strengths and weaknesses.

Strengths	Weaknesses
Highly differentiated and superior products that satisfy an important customer need.	High turnover in sales force in areas where competition is entrenched and/or where personal rapport with customer is critical.
Sufficient plant capacity to handle anticipated customer-demand and to capitalize on a back-order situation of a major competitor.	Late entry with a commodity or "me-too" product in a market segment that is in the mature or decline stage of development.
Patent or exclusive rights to a new product or manufacturing process.	Concept and product testing ineffective, resulting in the introduction of products that fail to satisfy customer needs.
Significant and favorable cost advantages in producing and/or distributing commodity-type products.	Insufficient depth in key management positions, resulting in prolonged interruptions to implementation of strategies when turnover in personnel occurs.
Larger and better trained sales force that allows business entity to maintain a more intensive personal selling campaign.	Unresolved labor dispute that is affecting productivity, and could result in plant shutdown.

An objective self-appraisal will pinpoint strengths that can be further enhanced and weaknesses that need to be corrected. It is important that a consensus understanding of the weaknesses be reached among management.

Goals and Objectives

Exhibit 39: Strategic Objectives—A Diversified Machinery Manufacturer

Definition: In the context of strategic planning, an objective is a goal toward which effort is directed—a competitive position to be attained, a target level of unit cost, or a degree of customer satisfaction, for example.

Characteristics:

1. An option often has two or three objectives because major business decisions often balance the immediate future with the longer term. Therefore, objectives of market penetration will be market share within specific profit, cost and time constraints.

2. Whether quantitative or qualitative, objectives must be measurable. For example, the objective of product differentiation is improved product quality as perceived by the customer. Improved product quality is measured through a customer survey, market share, or defect rates, for example.

3. Objectives should provide directional, not accounting, accuracy. Although objectives must be measurable, a numerical range rather than an exact number is usually preferable as well as more realistic.

4. A single objective may be predominant. Option objectives may be in conflict. If revenues cannot be increased without a decrease in profitability, a decision is required about which is more important.

5. Objectives should be relatively long-lived. Objectives should not change during the year because achievement of strategic options often requires more than one year of effort. Option objectives therefore should be changed only when major economic, technological or competitive events force a rethinking of the entire strategic plan.

ADDITIONAL EXHIBITS

Exhibit 40: Strategic Objectives—An Industrial Equipment Company

STRATEGIC OBJECTIVE STATEMENT	The *STRATEGIC OBJECTIVE STATEMENT* is a broad statement by the business manager which establishes the rationale for the specific goals and strategies proposed below. He should address how his competitive position will be altered by the plan, how this will be accomplished, and why this is a logical course for the business. He must communicate a clear concept of where the business is heading and of the full potential of the business before a thorough understanding of the strategies is possible. This statement must establish the *WHY* of the business plan.

GOALS	STRATEGIES	PROGRAMS
GOALS should focus on the major issues of importance or concern to the business. These issues might be found among the following: - Competitive actions - Cost position - Need for new products - Market growth - Product life cycle - Changing technology The stated goal should address the issue in a meaningful way. If increased competition is the issue, then a goal addressing this issue directly is more appropriate than, say, a sales-growth goal. The goal, statement should state *WHAT* we plan to accomplish in meeting the competitive challenge and the strategies should explain *HOW* we plan to achieve this goal. Only one to three principal goals should be stated here.	The *STRATEGIES* describe *HOW* we plan to accomplish our goals. *STRATEGY* is a statement of policy on: (a) How available resources will be deployed (b) How nonresource decisions will be made *STRATEGY* states what we are *GOING* to do—not what we *WANT* to do. *STRATEGY* is within the ability of the manager to implement. *STRATEGY* establishes a framework for making today's decisions.	All plans boil down to work that must be done and tasks that must be accomplished. Failure to define these tasks adequately and demonstrate commitment will destroy the credibility of the plan. The inability to define programs, timing and resource commitment means *there is no plan*. *PROGRAMS* identify the WHEN, WHERE and WHO of the business plan. *PROGRAMS* are specific work packages which must be accomplished to achieve a goal. *PROGRAMS* establish the commitment to accomplish a specific task by a specific time. The progress can be measured. *PROGRAMS* establish the resource commitments, responsibility and status. WITHOUT PROGRAM COMMITMENT, THE PLAN *CANNOT* BE TAKEN SERIOUSLY.

Exhibit 41: Strategic Objectives—A Computer Hardware and Services Corporation

INTRODUCTION

People and organizations are more likely to optimize achievement when clear objectives, or goals, have been established and communicated. These objectives are the minimum goals that must be achieved in order for a business to become what it has chosen to become. Objectives provide:

- Direction to the strategies necessary to achieve the objectives.
- Direction to the application of resources to these strategies.
- The basis for the measurement of future accomplishment.

Quantification is a necessity for measurement of results. Indicators such as sales, dollars and units of sales are easier to comprehend and more precise than terms denoting "better" or "worse." Even rating numbers make a statement more understandable (such as saying that "Our acceptance in the market is 4 but we want a rating of 7," or "Our training and development capabilities have a rating of 2, and we want a rating of 6").

THE NUMBER OF BUSINESS OBJECTIVES

Few organizations have been effective in accomplishing more than a limited number of truly strategic business objectives. Therefore, although more objectives may be appropriate for your organization, please focus on the most important in your strategic planning. WE RECOMMEND NO MORE THAN FIVE.

CATEGORIES OF BUSINESS OBJECTIVES

A common factor shared by all successful businesses is that each clearly understands the business opportunities and markets it has chosen to address, and the driving forces behind setting strategic objectives. These forces can be classified in three groups:

- Market driven: Objectives deriving from the overall markets and areas of those markets that appear most attractive in the planning period.
- Technology (know-how) driven: Objectives deriving from the technologies ("know-hows") that appear to hold promise in addressing the needs of your markets beyond the planning period.
- Other-forces driven: Objectives deriving from forces other than market and technology that drive the setting of strategic business objectives.

Classify each of your business objectives as falling into one of these three broad categories: market driven, technology ("know-how") driven, or other-forces driven. Then indicate the priorities of each of your top objectives in descending order of strategic importance.

LINKAGE OF OBJECTIVES TO STRATEGIES

After review of and concurrence with these objectives by senior corporate management, strategies to achieve these objectives will be detailed. These strategies will include consideration of the products or services to achieve the stated volume objectives, product or service development, making or buying, marketing, field service, and other strategies necessary to accomplish your objectives.

After defining your top strategic business objectives, you will be asked to summarize major changes from previous plans, provide financial results of your plan, and suggest any corporate-level changes in policy or practice that would favorably alter any of the above objectives.

Strategies

Exhibit 42: Statement of Strategy—A Diversified Industrial Equipment Corporation

Philosophy: Each division has been asked by the Chief Executive Officer to outline its business strategy based on the SBU (sector or company) strategy which was derived from the overall corporate strategy. The Division Strategy Statement will be the framework used to guide the division toward its objectives. This statement will be necessarily more detailed than the Sector Strategy Statement and will contain manufacturing, marketing, engineering and philosophical discussion of the approach used by the division in achieving its assigned role in the corporate structure. This entire process integrates corporate strategy directly with business strategy at the operating unit level.

Instructions:
- Based on the statement of business strategies submitted to and approved by the Chief Operating Officer, describe your division's five-year business strategy.

Discussion Points:
- Your division's business strategy will draw upon the strengths and weaknesses of your division functions, the characteristics of your division in the industry, and the market factors which influence your business. Comment only on those which are appropriate within the strategy statement of your business.
- For the oral review, you may wish to present the strategy in outline form for clarity.

Exhibit 43: Strategy Checklist—A Packaging Manufacturer

A. <u>Is the strategy consistent with the environment?</u>

1. Does your strategy address the critical issues?
2. Does the plan include creative thinking as opposed to being "more of the same"?
3. Have you evaluated the possible impact on your strategies of technological developments by your SBU, by your customers, competitors, suppliers and, especially, by those outside your industry?
4. Have you included the impact of cyclicality, if any, in your forecasts?
5. Have you given attention to how broader social and political trends might have an impact on total industry opportunities and threats?

B. <u>Market, customer and competitor analysis</u>

1. Are you satisfied that the SBU's served market is defined properly?
2. Have you examined the possibility of a change in the industry structure, i.e., the basic competitive nature and economics of the industry?
3. Does the plan reflect an assessment of the possible methods of segmenting the market?
4. Does the plan, to your satisfaction, describe how the SBU will successfully differentiate itself from its key competitors?
5. If you are planning to initiate a new strategy, does it represent the course that competitors would least expect?
6. Have you given adequate attention to probable competitive response to your planned strategic moves?
7. Does your strategy leave you vulnerable to the power of one major competitor, customer or supplier?
8. If the strategy is an imitation of the strategy of your most successful competitor, have the differences between your strengths and weaknesses and his been considered in determining the probable success of your strategy?
9. Is the timing of your implementation appropriate in light of what is known about market conditions?
10. How valid and complete is the information on which your strategy is based?
11. Does your strategy fit a niche in the market which is now filled by others? Is this niche likely to remain open to you for a long enough time to recover your capital investment plus earning an adequate return?
12. Have you given consideration to pricing as part of your total strategy? Given the rate of inflation in your costs, what differential rate of inflation will be necessary in your selling prices and what will the impact be?

(continued)

Exhibit 43: Strategy Checklist—A Packaging Manufacturer (continued)

   13. Have the real reasons why customers buy from you been discovered? Are they likely to change in the future?
   14. Have you identified your major competitors, determined who their major customers are and the competitive advantage this suggests?
   15. Has the cost structure of each major competitor been estimated? What relative strengths and weaknesses does this suggest?

C. Does the strategy fit the stage of the product life cycle?
   1. Does the strategy fit the life cycle of the product(s) involved (development, growth, shakeout, maturity, saturation)?
   2. Does your strategy involve the production of a new product, the use of a new technology, and/or the entry into a new market? If so, have you really assessed the risks and the requirements for successful implementation?

D. Is the strategy consistent with your internal policies, styles of management, philosophy and operating procedures?
   1. Is your strategy explicit and understood by all those responsible for executing it?
   2. Is your strategy consistent with the objectives and policies of your organization?
   3. Are your supporting objectives and strategies consistent with your strategic intention?
   4. Are all supporting objectives and strategies mutually consistent?
   5. Does the strategy exploit your strengths and avoid your major weaknesses? Does it concentrate your strengths against your competitors' weaknesses?
   6. Is your organizational structure consistent with your strategy?
   7. Is the strategy consistent with the objectives and strategies of the corporation?

E. Is the strategy in line with your resources?
   1. Capital
      a. Is your cash flow consistent with the strategic intention assigned to this SBU in the past?
      b. Does your strategy embody the concept of economy—are you planning to succeed at any cost or at the minimum cost?
      c. Have full considerations been given to the financial consequences on this SBU, if the requested capital allocations are made?
      d. Have all the investment requirements necessary to support successful implementation of your strategy been included in the financial projection for the SBU?
   2. Technology
      a. Do you have, or will you have, adequate technology to permit realization of the strategy?
      b. Does your strategy result in the identification of solvable problems?
      c. Has an evaluation of potential new technologies (substitutes) been conducted?
   3. Manpower
      a. Do you have, or will you have, the sufficient manpower to realize your strategy?
   4. Supplies
      a. Have you considered future supply (materials and energy) constraints and possible alternate sources, both in general and by geographic region?

(continued)

Exhibit 43: Strategy Checklist—A Packaging Manufacturer (continued)

    b. Has the impact of future cost increases in materials and energy been included in forecasted constant-dollar margins?

    c. Are you satisfied that proper action plans have been developed so that future, adverse supplier pricing actions can be mitigated as much as practicable?

F. <u>Are the risks in pursuing the strategy acceptable?</u>

1. Do you have too much capital and management tied into this strategy in light of the SBU's matrix position?
2. To what extent is the success of your strategy dependent upon displacing a well-established competitor?
3. Is the payback period acceptable in light of potential environmental change?
4. Does the strategy take you too far from your current products, markets and capabilities? Is it the right risk for you?
5. Has the strategy been tested with appropriate risk analysis, such as sensitivity analysis?

G. <u>Contingency plans</u>

1. Have you developed alternative plans for achieving your strategic intention in light of changing circumstances and differing competitive response?
2. Will the contingency plans allow you to keep the initiative or are they merely an across-the-board cutback (retreat)?

H. <u>Some frequent strategy mistakes</u>

1. Betting on long shots.
2. Trying for a "turnaround" in an unpromising situation.
3. Not believing your good luck and thereby failing to capitalize on competitors' errors.
4. Wounding a competitor without seriously crippling him.
5. Precipitating a collapse while attempting to harvest the business.
6. Excessive marketing and R&D when the SBU is weak, and insufficient marketing and R&D when strong.
7. Risking major trouble for little prospective gain.
8. Inadequate attention to the history of the SBU and the industry it is in, especially with respect to defining the limits of the possible.
9. Confronting a competitor on his own ground and on his own terms.
10. Biting off more than you can chew. Don't exhaust the confidence of your organization in a vain effort.
11. Failure to develop a strategy that is flexible and adaptable to changing circumstances.
12. Persisting in the same competitive strategy, with additional resources, in spite of initial failure.
13. Forgetting that business strategy represents the means to an economic end and that economic objectives must govern business strategy.
14. Preoccupation with developing tactical efficiency at the expense of strategic thinking.
15. Failure to consciously choose the competitor whom you wish to challenge.
16. Failure to reexamine an apparently stable environment and thereby mistakenly perceive a strategic challenge as merely a tactical challenge.
17. Failure to recognize an opportunity presented by a changing environment.

Exhibit 44: Statement of Strategy—A Food Company

Description of Strategies —After stating your objectives, you should describe the strategies you propose to follow which will allow you to accomplish the objectives stated for the business unit.

THIS IS THE MOST IMPORTANT SECTION OF YOUR WRITTEN PLAN AND WOULD BE EXPECTED TO OCCUPY THE MOST SPACE . Your description should identify the important elements of the strategy and explain them in enough detail to allow corporate management to evaluate the overall strategy. The specific elements your description should cover may include such projects as new products, new markets, new pricing, new distribution and new promotion, acquisitions, divestment or pruning activities.

In general, your strategies will be evaluated on the basis of the following criteria:

- Consistency with internal strengths and weaknesses.
- Consistency with external economic, political, technological and social environment.
- Consistency with established corporate policy.
- Consistency with longer-term strategic growth goals of the company.
- Sufficiency of challenge of the overall strategic position.
- Level of new investment requirements.
- Degree of risk.

Action Programs

Exhibit 45: Action Plans—A Consumer and Industrial Products Company

Action plans provide a specific outline of WHAT , WHERE , WHEN and HOW resources will be deployed to implement strategies. Action plans also indicate WHO is responsible for the execution of each segment and the date it will be completed.

An example of an Action Plan that supports a strategy to withdraw from unprofitable markets might be:

1. Analyze all markets being served to measure levels of past profitability — J. Smith — 8/15/83
2. Forecast profit potential by market area (1984-1990) and report to General Manager those yielding a return on sales below 12%. — J. Jones — 8/25/83
3. Recommend markets for withdrawal and scheduled dates. — H. Miller — 9/25/83
4. Coordinate with Transportation and Product Distribution Personnel and Group Administration. — H. Miller — 10/15/83

Exhibit 46: Action Plans—A Machinery and Tool Manufacturer

Principal Action Programs should include any major new programs currently active in the business unit or planned to start during the planning period. Fully describe each program and its role in the strategic plan of the unit. Text should address such items as type and size of target market, competitive position in the market, technical and market risk, external factors prompting the program (OSHA, EPA, etc.). Include the program's goals (specific and measurable), how long it will take, and why it is feasible. If the program includes the introduction of new products, discuss an approximate estimate of incremental sales and profits. "Incremental" includes sales and profits which would otherwise have been lost if the program were not carried out.

Critical Milestones are those things we must accomplish without fail (e.g., attain a viable market share, achieve acceptable financial returns, demonstrate grasp of a particularly vital technology, prevent our customers from integrating, etc.). This should focus and summarize our effort in the half dozen or less issues which drive our future. Those, if met, should fulfill our strategies and objectives.

Milestones must be specific, tangible and allow for determination of whether an action has been successful and timely. Actions are required to implement a strategy. A strategy may have one or several key elements. Each should have specific actions backing it up. From the statement of strategy, each required strategic action should be segregated and the associated milestones should be indicated, as shown on the example.

Example (Hypothetical Business Unit)

Actions	Success	Minimum Acceptable	Absolute Failure	Date
Achieve viable market share in widgets	15%	10%	7%	Jan. '81
ROA—before tax—Widget Division	20%	15%	10%	Jan. '81
Prevent oil company integration of widgets	Exxon, Mobil, Texaco unintegrated 1983	Any two unintegrated 1983	Two or more integrated 1983	Sept. '84
Demonstrate new widget technology	Lab & field tested successfully by 1979	Lab tested successfully by 1981	Neither by 1982	As shown

A milestone schedule is a summary of what we must attain, but is not a mere rehash of action plans or financial objectives. Some of those items we can fail on; yet emerge an overall winner: Others we can greatly overachieve on, yet lose the game. How will we score ourselves; what is the crux of the matter? At the point where we admit failure to achieve a milestone, what strategy should be adopted?

Principal action programs and their respective milestones should be prepared for the entire five-year planning period. Furthermore, the programs and milestones for 1984 should be detailed to the point that they can be measured and implemented as part of next year's Profit Incentive Plan.

Exhibit 47: Action Plan Summary—A Building Products Company

ACTION PROGRAM SUMMARY[1]

_____
Strategic Business Unit

Description of Program[2]	Issues Addressed[3]	Tasks[4]	$ Resources Required (000's)[5]	Target Date[6] Begin End	Responsibility[7]
1.		1a.	$		
		1b.	$		
		1c.	$		
2.		2a.	$		
		2b.	$		
		2c.	$		
etc.		etc.	etc.		

_____

[1] For <u>major</u> programs only. Maximum of fifteen for the five-year plan period. Major action programs are those that address the issues. These can be marketing programs, manufacturing programs, R&D programs, human resources, etc., capital or expense. Additional schedules may be used if needed.

[2] Briefly describe the program.

[3] Indicate by number the issue that this program addresses. If a program addresses more than one issue, indicate the numbers of those issues from [previous portion of the plan].

[4] Itemize the important activities of the program (i.e., the key tasks in how the program is to be accomplished).

[5] For each task listed, indicate the dollar resources required, capital or expense. NOTE: Cost of manpower should be included only to the extent that it represents an incremental cost (i.e., you added staff specifically for the program).

[6] For each task listed, indicate the month and year that the activity will begin and the month and year that it will be completed.

[7] Name of operating or staff function directly responsible for the task (i.e., finance, sales, R&D, personnel, etc.).